MW01241712

Fathers

Fathers

a memoir

Dave Donelson

FATHERS

A memoir

Copyright © 2020 by Dave Donelson.

All Rights Reserved. Published and printed in the United States of America by Donelson SDA, Inc. No part of this book may be reproduced, copied or used in any form or manner whatsoever without written permission, except in the case of brief quotations in reviews and critical articles.

For information, contact Donelson SDA, Inc.

44 Park Lane, West Harrison, NY 10604

FIRST EDITION

Disclaimer : Some of this work is semi-fiction and all events described herein are remembered or imagined, including settings, dialogue, and characters. Any similarity to real persons, entities, or companies is purely dependent on the author's admittedly flawed memory of circumstances and events from many years ago. Real brand names, company names, names of public personalities or real people may be employed for credibility because they are part of our culture and everyday lives. Regardless of context, their use is meant neither as endorsement nor criticism: such names are used fictitiously without intent to describe their actual conduct or value. Many other names, products or brands are inventions of the author's imagination. Donelson SDA, Inc. and its directors, employees, distributors, retailers, wholesalers and assigns disclaim any liability or responsibility for the author's statements, words, ideas, criticisms or observations. Donelson SDA, Inc., assumes no responsibility for errors, inaccuracies, or omissions.

The Ideal

This is where I came from.
I passed this way.
This should not be shameful
Or hard to say.

A self is a self.
It is not a screen.
A person should respect
What he has been.

This is my past
Which I shall not discard.
This is the ideal.
This is hard.

--James Fenton
Out of Danger, 1994

TABLE OF CONTENTS

1984

For Jeremy and Leigh Anna

Foreword
with explanations but no apologies

This book has been hiding in the niches of my mind for quite some time. What finally prompted me to start writing it was seeing my grandson, Steve, grow from a toddler to a little manchild. Along with that came the realization that there are big swaths of my life that Steve's father, my son Jeremy, doesn't know much about, or at least he doesn't know my version of them, and I'd like him to hear it from me. I don't know if my story matters to them, but I like to think it does.

Most of this book is about my early life and the events and people that stand out in my memories of it. Many things, including my various careers, later friendships, struggles, and accomplishments aren't part of the story. I am also not writing about my loving wife Nora for several reasons, but mostly because our precious oneness is nobody else's business. She is beautiful and supportive and wonderful, which is all I need say about her aside from thanking her for putting up with me through the writing of this book.

I also want to thank Nina Little, my second cousin, who provided a great deal of family history and genealogy that I couldn't have done without.

A reader of memoirs usually expects the author to accomplish a straightforward task: tell what happened as well as he can remember. But it's not that easy. Memory at best is flawed and at worst a liar. I try to write as truly as I can, but I cannot guarantee that this book contains nothing but absolute fact. Most of these events happened many, many years ago. Mists of time and all that. I was also a child when much of it took place. An observant, intelligent child I like to think, but still not fully informed when it came to understanding much of what happened and who did what to whom. My ability to tell the good guys from the bad guys was no better than most kids', which is to say I was easily fooled. My first stepfather, Walt, for example, was an enthusiastic participant in manly arts like baseball and beery socializing and had no flaws as far as I could see. What I didn't understand, due to my age at the time, was that he could do all these fun things because he didn't bother to hold down a job. He didn't wear a black hat, so I didn't identify him as a villain until much later when I witnessed some of the things he did to my mother. It's hard to say today what is fact and what is a bleak reflection of ugly fable.

The reader should know, too, that many of my reflections on life are viewed through a scree of alcohol. I drank heavily from my early teens to the age of 46. That makes for over three decades of details that come and go in my memory and certainly affects my recollections of the childhood I had before booze washed over me. I'm sober now, but much granular detail of my past was drowned in alcohol.

A few other warnings: this is not a chronological story. The memories I draw on are all jumbled in my head and that's more or less the way they are presented. Also, I remember and write in a variety of forms and styles— prose, poetry, re-imagined dialog, different narrative voices and points of view, so some readers may find the work incoherent in places. So be it. That's the way the stories live in my head so that's the way they came out on paper.

Some parts of this book read as fiction, but they are as true as any of the staunchly-researched fact-based accounts. The events depicted may have been compressed, exaggerated, or warped, but the feelings they evoke for me, at least, are as real as the oak tree outside my window. And that's how I hope the reader accepts them. My memories may be distorted, but the feelings I try to convey are perfectly valid and as real as I can express them. The point of writing after all, isn't to merely record the facts about events and people. It's to discover the ever-widening ripples of those facts after they're tossed into the pond of time.

In my memory, my fathers stand in file before me. My last father is first in line and in this book; I spent more years coping with him and hate him the most. Second is my birth father. His figure is indistinct in my vision because there is a void where we could have been together but weren't. I don't so much miss him as wonder about what could have been. Last in line before me is my second father; I hate him for what he did to my mother and brothers at a time when I was too young to protect them.

In the background stands a line of grandfathers great and small. They are legends to me, mythic figures in family tales told and retold by the women who raised me. One charms the world with his fiddle and his smile. Another never walked when he could run and worked hard and screwed hard even into his dotage. Others stand in that line, their outlines hazy and impermanent. They are names, not people.

In yet another line stands my son and his son, my daughter, and perhaps other sons and daughters to come. For I am a father, too; one of a continuum of men in my family leaning into, shadowing, shoving, shaping, steering, staining each other through the generations. We saw, square, plane, and sand each other until, like raw planks turned into rough furniture, our imperfections are hidden, only to bloom through the varnish again just as knots bleed from the wood with the passage of time. Like distracted craftsmen, though, our actions are not always thought through or even purposeful, although they are always our own. We are both heroes and pariahs, role models and villains. What I did to my children I did both intentionally and accidentally, for bad or for good, with regret or with pride, but I will never deny responsibility for any of it.

I am a father.

Jack Donelson, 1950

Three

Fathers

Lou, c 1991

Lou

It is Lou's fault when Mom gets arrested. It is his fault because my stepfather has dominated our lives, forcing us to listen for his heavy footsteps, to dodge his anger, to shut up and never talk back to him. It is his fault she did what she did because he gave us nothing but the bare minimum. I am used to that, but this is too much for me. My love for my mother lies close under my skin, easily inflamed. Enough is enough and it's too much this time. At last, I threaten to kill him.

Lou is bigger than me. Not taller, but thicker, with a deep chest like a buffalo and biceps built by hours of auto body work, pounding and bending steel and manhandling heavy air wrenches. He rolls up his T-shirt sleeves like a James Dean wannabe and has a well-earned beer belly that is hard, not flabby. He has a smart-ass grin some find endearing but they don't see his private face, which relaxes into a resentful pout. He smokes cigarillos, tiny, almost effeminate cigars with plastic tips. I saw his strength when I was younger and I was afraid of him then. Now, I am grown and I am angry.

When my phone rang that morning, the last thing I expected to hear was my mother crying. "I'm going to be in the newspaper, David," she sobbed. Before I could ask why, more words tumble out. "I got caught

3

stealing. I snuck some underpants into my purse and they caught me." My mother is a shoplifter.

I rush to the house and find her red-eyed and smoking a cigarette at the kitchen table. Lou is in the garage.

"I am so embarrassed, David," she says. Before I can ask, she explains. "I needed some underwear and I didn't want to ask him."

"Ask him? Ask him what?"

"For money. I didn't have any. I never have any." She takes an angry drag on her cigarette. "I am so tired of needing it all the time." I calm her as best I can and tell her she should come to me for money. If Lou won't support her, I will. "I know that," she answers. "But I don't want to have to ask you, either. If I wasn't so stupid and useless, I'd have a job and wouldn't have to ask anyone for anything."

That isn't right, but I can't argue with her when she's in that state. Why should a woman who gives so much to her family need to beg support from them? If she is a partner in the marriage, why doesn't she get any sustenance from it? When she finally calms down, I go grim-faced to the garage.

He and I come to this moment of truth because Lou refuses to give Mom money for anything beyond necessities unless she begs for it or, even better, earns it by laboring for him in his backyard garage. As far as he is concerned, his job as the provider for the family is done when he bestows upon her a grocery allowance and pays the mortgage and the utility bills. Anything else is pure extravagance unless it's for something he wants, like a trip to Daytona for the stock car races. If she needs money for back-to-school clothes or doctor visits, she has to beg for it.

For years, Mom swallowed her pride and we got by with patched blue jeans, hand-me-down shirts, and socks she darned on a wooden egg with needle and thread. She barbered our hair herself to save a dollar, each of us taking our turn sitting in the kitchen, shirtless with a towel around our shoulders, while she snipped away. We saw a dentist only when there was a toothache that lasted more than a couple of days and a doctor only when absolutely necessary, since we got our exams and shots for school at the town's charity clinic. At Christmas, we each were allowed to pick one gift from the Sears catalogue, a process that took days and days. Mom made it as fun as she could, but it was not joyful.

It was not the poverty that hurt—we'd never known anything else—but Lou rubbed our faces in it every day. He was not poor, but we were. He had a good job with a decent lower-middle-class income, union benefits, and a pension, but that was his, not ours, and he never let us forget that our life was nothing until he came into it. My resentment for that mindset has driven me throughout my life.

It was not Mom's fault that we were poor. She was not educated but she was smart. She was socially timid but brave at heart; not assertive but very, very stubborn. She always did what she needed to do to survive and take care of my brothers and me. She didn't drive when we lived in Kansas City so she hauled me and later my brother Wayne around with her in an old red wagon to do her grocery shopping and visit the library. Walt, her husband before Lou, worked only sporadically and drank most of what he earned, so Mom took in ironing from the neighbor ladies to put food on our table. She made sure we never missed any meals but we ate a lot of navy beans and noodles flavored with a bit of ham hock or ox tail.

Mom may have married Walt out of concern that I needed a father after she and Jack, my natural father, were divorced. That was probably not the only reason, though, since Walt was a good-time ladies' man she met while living and working at her mother's tavern, a place she intensely disliked. But that is certainly why she married Lou after she left Walt and why she stayed with him until he died. When she met Lou, she was a young mother with no job skills or prospects. What she did have, though, were three kids, one of them a disabled baby, who needed a home. Lou was a charming meal ticket at first but soon turned into the abusive, penny-pinching bully who brought home nothing but a paycheck.

Once they were married, Mom scrimped pin money from her grocery allowance, but when she needed more, Lou didn't give it to her; he hired her to earn "extra" money just like Wayne and I did, by working for him in the garage. He paid me a dollar an hour to prep cars for painting by wet-sanding them in his backyard body shop. Mom got the same for detailing the cars, bending herself into pretzel shapes to reach interior crevices with a vacuum and scrub brushes. It was nasty work that led to years of back pain she tried to relieve at the hands of chiropractic quacks and later with legitimate surgery that was only partly successful.

When it came to me, Lou made no bones about having no use for a skinny middle-schooler with glasses whose nose was always in a book instead of under the hood of a car. I was twelve when he married Mom and moved us into the first single-family house I'd ever lived in. I got no allowance for chores since mowing the lawn and raking leaves and carrying out the trash was the labor he demanded I give to him for my bed in his house and my meals on his table.

One blistering summer day not long after we move into the house on Jackson Street, Lou tells me to close my book and get to work.

"Didn't I tell you to cut them weeds behind the garage?" he says.

I look up. "Yes, but I just want to finish this chapter."

"Finish it later. I want them weeds cut right now."

"But the sun's around there. Can't I wait until it's shady?"

"Now, you little son-of-a-bitch. I said NOW!"

Lou is big, at least to me, because I am small and skinny. Once, when he and I are repairing the transmission on my first car, we put the car up on blocks so he could slide underneath on a creeper and manhandle the transmission onto his chest before wriggling out from under the car with it. It must have weighed two hundred pounds. On a hot day like this one, he may drink a case of Schlitz. His smile can be charming but today I see his smirk, which isn't.

He clamps his hand around my skinny arm and yanks me up out of the chair. He pushes me through the kitchen and shoves me out the back door. His rock-hard grip leaves purple welts on my arm, but they fade in the sun behind the garage.

I swing the cutter whip into the weed stems standing tall and tangled in the hot sun. I don't know why I am cutting them down; they don't obstruct anything in the narrow strip of dirt between the garage and the gravel alley running behind it. But Lou wants it done, so I do it. Tall, white-juiced milkweed, sticky thistles, tough-stemmed Johnson grass. Who was Johnson, I wonder, and why did he have grass named after him? He must have been a mean man.

I swing the whip again and again. It has a flat blade set at an angle on a flexible steel shaft with a wooden handle and it gets heavier with every swing. It is slow, hard, hot work. The saw-toothed leaves scratch my arms. The stiff weed stems snap around my fingers when the blade slashes through them. Gravel dust from the alley coats the leaves and puffs into the air along with the grasshoppers who flee the whip, whirring before the flashing blade to new hiding places in the brush. The sun glares off the white siding of the garage. In a book, it would be sun glaring off the icy sea, the hot gravel dust would be smoke from a cannon battle, the weeds whirring warriors with stabbing knives.

"Watch the blade. Watch your leg. Don't cut off your toes," I say to myself as I swing the whip. "If you chop off your foot, he'll just laugh at you." Swish, thunk. Swish, thunk. I am not quite strong enough to drive the blade all the way through the stiff weeds in one stroke, but every time I swing, a few more fall.

"Watch what you're doing," I repeat.

Swish, thunk. Swish, thunk. Swish, thunk. I am in a place I don't want to be. Somewhere in a book, horse-hair plumes fly on helmets and shields flash blinding sun into enemy eyes. Swish, thunk. Swish, CLINK, BANG. The blade drives a piece of gravel into the garage--I had swung too low.

"Watch it, stupid," I mutter.

The whip grows heavy in my sweaty hand. Sticky sap spots my scratched arms and dust coats my sun-reddened skin. I finish the job and gasp for breath in the thick air as I drag the whip back up the hill to the house.

"Did you rake it up? When I go down there, I better find them weeds in a pile," Lou demands.

"I will. I just need a drink of water."

"You're a lazy son of a . . ." Lou starts, but he is interrupted by Mom coming outside with a glass of cool water.

"He's going to have a sunstroke," she protests while keeping an eye on Lou's expression. I gulp the water down and she adds, "And look at his skin. Jesus, he's all sun-burnt."

"He ain't hurt none," Lou answers. To me, he says, "Those weeds need to be piled up so I can burn them."

Mom brushes her hand across my brow, wiping away the sweat and gravel dust and flakes of weed. I shiver under her cool touch. She takes the glass from my hand and goes back in the house. I start to follow, but Lou stops me.

"Let me see your arm," he says loudly so Mom can hear him as she goes through the door. "How bad are you burnt?" He takes my wrist and yanks the arm out straight for inspection. The screen door slams behind him and he slaps my sunburned forearm with his fingers. I gasp between my clenched teeth. "Don't look too bad," the grins, examining his white finger marks on my red skin. He smacks the forearm again, harder, and a weak mewling escapes from me as I shudder from the pain. "You little son of a bitch," he snarls. He slaps my arm three times, hard and fast, then drops my wrist and walks away.

I slump and silently cradle my screaming arm. I won't cry out to Mom; she can't help. I can only cringe over my fiery arm. I suck it up, leave the grass whip where it lays, and fetch a rake to finish the job.

Over the years, Mom tries to defend him by telling me that Lou doesn't know what to make of me, but that is not true. He makes clear exactly what he thinks of me and people like me. After my high school graduation, Lou tells me I have to pay rent to live in his house (never "our house"). Mom finally talks him out of it since I am going to college, something I will pay for myself, and he acquiesces grudgingly. My brother Wayne escapes the house as soon as he can. College isn't an option for him, so he pays rent until he moves out not long after he gets his high school diploma. Once I marry and leave the house, I finish college, start a family, and launch a white-collar career, proving him wrong in all his red-neck beliefs. Bullies don't always win, the deck isn't automatically stacked against you, and who you know isn't the only path to success. I privately celebrate when I accidentally see his income tax return not long after I go into TV ad sales; I pay more in taxes that year than he has earned from both his job as a fireman and from his backyard

9

body shop. It is a small, petty victory I never boast about, but I revel in it.

Mom makes a home for Ken, my mentally-impaired youngest brother, stepping in when Lou gets too nasty with him and doing what she can to give him a decent, productive life. She does so as long as she lives, getting up at five AM to roust him out of bed for work, fixing his lunch, washing his clothes, looking after him as she always has. She blames herself for his disability, although that's totally unjustified. Her guilt isn't what drives her to care for him, though. He is her son, and he needs her; that all she cares about. She would do the same for Wayne or me.

After I am married and gone, Mom and Lou move to a larger house. It has a bigger garage so he can work on more than one car at a time, which is the rationale for the move. Somehow he miraculously comes up with the money to install a small in-ground swimming pool. The house and pool, of course, are things he wants, so somehow he could find the money for them just as he could always afford a used Corvette to play with while Mom buys our bread at the day-old bakery.

Lou stands at the workbench tinkering with a carburetor clamped in the bench vice. He sees me come in, but doesn't look up. I stop an arm's length away and speak to the side of his face. I've grown up and he's gotten older. He's still bigger than me, his hands and arms still powerful, but my anger is bigger yet.

"You know why she did it?" I demand.

He doesn't look up from the bench. "Yeah, I know," he answers. I can tell he is watching me out of the corner of his eye. His fingers keep moving a screwdriver around the carburetor, but he isn't really doing anything with it. "If she needed money, all she had to do was ask."

"She shouldn't have to ask, goddammit," I snap. "You better start giving her money of her own. You better stop making her beg for it."

He turns to look at me, surprise on his face that I would be telling him what to do. There's maybe a little fear in his expression, too. I can see him sizing me up, calculating just how mad I am. He doesn't put the screwdriver down but I don't back away. I don't blink, either.

"Let me make this very simple," I say. "If you can't make enough money to provide for her, I will." It was the most insulting thing that came to my mind. He let his eyes drop. There is a hammer lying on the bench but he's not looking at it.

"She'll be all right," he says.

"She better be," I say, lowering my voice and speaking very slowly and very clearly, a tactic I had learned on the school debate team. It makes the audience listen carefully to every word. "If I ever find out she needs to beg you for money again, I'll kill you."

The threat pops out on its own and surprises even me, but I mean it. Lou knows it, too, and turns quickly back to the workbench without saying anything. I don't know what else to say or do, so I leave.

The next day, the piece in the newspaper is so small no one ever notices it and the judge lets Mom go with a warning after she apologizes to the store. None of us ever mentions it again. It isn't necessary.

Years later, the day of Lou's funeral, Wayne and I sit at the kitchen table and laugh and laugh. We don't laugh at family stories or dredge up humorous anecdotes about the good old days gone by. We laugh because the son-of-a-bitch who called us sons-of-bitches is dead and we have survived him.

Jack, 1951

Jack

My birth father, Jack Donelson, is largely a cipher in my life. Neither of my stepfathers filled the vacuum he left, nor did they think to try. They were men and they were there, but they weren't my father. Jack was there, sometimes, but he was not a very strong presence. My earliest memories of him are from when we lived in Kansas City, as did he. He picked me up every other Sunday and took me to his home so we could spend the day together. I passed the day following him around while he did various chores and projects. Out of politeness, I played with my younger half-brother Mike, a whiney little twerp. We paid an occasional visit to my grandparents in St. Joseph. When I got a little older, we went fishing and I watched him build stuff in his basement workshop.

Jack did teach me some things; probably more than I realize. The odd lesson comes back to me now and then. Like every time I pick up a push broom to sweep my shop, I remember him telling me to not lean into it so hard; if you stand upright and push it methodically, the broom will do the work. He spoke from experience gained as a school janitor, which was the only job I ever knew him to have.

For a year or two, he was the janitor at Scarritt School in Kansas City, my elementary school. As an adult, I wondered if he had asked to be assigned there. Whether it was coincidental or not, I was proud to see him cleaning in the halls or stepping into the classroom with his toolbox. One of my clearest memories of him is when he was summoned to the nurse's office to help me deal with my first loose tooth. It dangled in my mouth but wouldn't fall out on its own. I refused to let anyone touch it despite the blood that filled my mouth and scared me witless. Jack came in and knelt in front of me with a tissue in his hand.

"Let me wipe some of this off so I can see your mouth," he said, dabbing at the blood welling out of my lips. "Now open up so I can see." Calmed by his steady demeanor, I obeyed. Before I knew what had happened, he held the tooth in the bloody tissue. "That wasn't so bad, was it?" he said. "Next time, you can do it yourself, can't you?" I nodded.

A couple of years later, probably just before we decamped for St. Joseph, he picked me up and headed for his house. "You know," he said apropos of nothing a few minutes into the drive, "a man is known by how clean his teeth and shoes are." I looked down at my shoes and, sure enough, they were pretty scuffed up. I ran my tongue over my teeth and my shortcomings in that department were apparent, too. If he had been a full time presence in my life, I wonder what else he might have taught me.

I don't really know anything about Mom's relationship with him. "He had big shoulders and looked sharp in his uniform," was all she ever said about how they met in the Ko-Z-Inn. He'd served in the navy in the Pacific in World War II and didn't see much action but apparently came home with a smile that could win over a teenage waitress dying to get away from her job tending tables for her mother. They wed and I was conceived shortly thereafter but the marriage didn't last more than a few months after I was born.

Jack came to my high school graduation and my wedding to Eileen,

14

although I can't recall seeing him at either one. I do, however, remember my college commencement. He found me after the ceremony and congratulated me and told me he was very proud. He also gave me an elegant-looking ballpoint pen that I carried for many years. Eventually the clip broke and it disappeared in a desk drawer someplace.

Jack seemed healthy to me, but he was actually little more than a husk of his former robust self by the time I was old enough to know him. He had been afflicted by an illness that sapped his strength and nearly cost him his life until it was finally diagnosed correctly: adult-onset juvenile diabetes. Once the doctors figured out what it was and put him on a diet and insulin therapy, he recovered, but not before significant damage had been done. He died at 42 from heart failure. I am sure, now, that the battle with his health kept us apart for considerable stretches of time. If he had been a full-time father, I imagine we would have been closer. I try not to dwell on the missed possibilities because thinking about them makes me sad.

I don't know much about Jack as a man, I am ashamed to say. I mean, I know what he did for a living and how he died, I know he re-married and had another son, but I don't know much else about him. The timeline of my life has a huge blank space where he should be in the years from when Mom left Walt to the point where I got married. Jack was my father yet I did not know him. Two pieces of anemic advice and an electroplated ballpoint aren't much of a legacy. I sense he wanted to give me more but either I was too distant to take it or the opportunity was lost in the chaos that was my early life.

With Grandma Donelson (Goldie)

For He Gave

The Pieta glows rosy pink in the Sunday sunrise as Mary weeps over her wasted son.

Shuffle on by them we go with the crowd softly chatting its way into the dim sanctuary.

Shuffle, shuffle, flowers on hats and striped ties on white shirts and hair cream glistening.

Shuffle, shuffle to the pews.

Faces to backs of heads, paper fans flap through the close-in air.

Sit, sing, bow our heads

Listen, stand, sit, pay, pray, sing doxology and recite Apostle's Creed.

Shuffle, shuffle out past the pink Pieta and onto the summer-sticky parking lot.

~~§~~

I go with Jack, my father, to his mother's house where I change into my good play clothes and follow him into the basement. There he will teach me how to skin a squirrel. It is dark but he pulls the string on the light and I am blinded by the sudden flash, a sun that explodes in my eyes like I imagine death erupted in the squirrel's head when he shot him. My eyes clear and I see the dead squirrels in the basket at the end of the work table. Just chop off the head and paws, slide off the slippery skin, and slit the belly to slip out the entrails. Wrap the bloody parts all up in the fur. Set the meat and bones aside for dinner. Keep the tail, though, you could use that on your bike or something someday. He shows me how, then I do it. When we finish there is very little blood considering the entire basket was full of little tawny creatures that had been shot just that morning before church.

~~§~~

After my allotted time with we him, we leave.

Through many miles of dangerous city, he drives me home or

Wherever we go.

As the day wears, the wheels crunch over the pavement and he drives me through clouds of stinking bus fumes.

Halfway home,

"There are two things you should know," he says.

I don't answer; he doesn't expect me to by now.

"You need a shine on your shoes and

on your pearly whites, too."

I still don't say anything, but I look at my scruffy shoes and run my tongue over my furry teeth.

"People look at things like that. They judge you that way. You know what I mean?"

He is only partly right, of course, just like he is only partly there some of the time and not there at all most of the time.

Some years later, we try to camp.

He builds a plywood box and fills it with food and cutlery and a kerosene stove and puts it in the pickup truck which is his fantasy marked "and sons." There is only one real son, my half-brother Mike from my stepmother, plus me, whatever I am every other week. He puts the row boat on top by himself because I am too short and weak. We drive to the lake, taking the plywood box and the tent and my copy of *Ivanhoe*. First the highway, then the gravel, then the dirt road; finally we reach the outer frustrations where it is raining. We pitch the tent, he and I, while Mike whines in the cab of the truck.

The tent will leak if I touch it from the inside while it is raining outside, he tells me. That makes no sense but I believe him anyway because he is my father. I read *Ivanhoe* while he fumes about the dreary rain.

The next day, he has a grand plan for bait, but the seine doesn't catch any minnows so we dig worms and put them in the coffee can with mud where they drown in the wet dirt. I try to cast his red and white wooden bass plug. It scares me. I foresee its deadly gang hooks piercing my thumb if he jerks the line while I hold the lure. One point digs through to scrape the bone. The other flesh-rips the soft skin on the back of my hand with the barb through my freckles. It peels back the meat but no blood comes, just me going white while he jerks and yanks it closer. Outside my imagination in the real world, I cast a stiff metal fishing rod. The reel whirs. The plug flies. The line snarls in tangles and tiny knots. The red and white wooden bass plug splashes into the lily pads.

"He jumped right up and he said, I'm glad I'm just a little green frog, swimming in the water. Glump, glump, glump."

He takes a turn of line around his hand and yanks hard, hard, so very hard that the line slices his flesh and he bleeds. He snatches a knife from his belt and cuts the line. Sad, so sad, pitying faces fill the sky. They reflect back from between the lily pads.

That night around the campfire he shows me a broomstick topped with a green steel spearhead with two points. Neptune had one, I say.

"A gig?" he asks.

Cocky, I answer, "A trident."

"For frogs?"

"For stirring storms and parting the waters," I answer.

"No," he dismisses me, "that was someone else."

We float through the bulrushes in the dark. I shine the light to find red frog eyes. Could he? Whoosh—stab! No!

In the morning light he dangles a hook with red yarn but the daytime-yellow frog's eyes just stare, never blinking, never crying. One finally bites and snags and dangles, bleeding on the string. He cuts the lips to free the hook but the legs are too small to eat.

It isn't time to go until the next day but *Ivanhoe* is finished and it rains inside the tent because I touch it just to see what happens, so we roll up the seine with the gig and the metal fishing pole and pack up the plywood box with the food and the cutlery and the stove and put it all in the truck and drive home. They to his; me to mine. No talk.

Much, much later, at my college graduation, I don't even know he is there until after I get my diploma, the caps and gowns and the shuffle down and up the aisle. He emerges from the crowd to lay a hand on my shoulder in the sunshine. He hands me a gold ballpoint pen in a box. Cost him sixty dollars--more than I paid for my first car. More than three weeks rent. More than he could ever afford.

Goldie (Grandma) Donelson, Carl (Grandpa) Donelson,
(Aunt) Nancy, (Uncle) Billy, 1952

With Wayne on Garner Avenue, c 1960

Walt

When she finally has enough of my stepfather Walt, Mom enlists my two almost-grown cousins to load our stuff into a U-Haul trailer and bring it from our tenement apartment in Kansas City to the cellar of my grandmother's tavern in St. Joseph. We move as soon as school lets out for the summer. Walt will be surprised to find us gone when he comes home from wherever he goes during the day while other fathers are working. The move is a shock to me, too, because it means I can't go to Safety Guard camp that summer and train to exercise the immense authority that comes from wearing a white Sam Browne belt and wielding a stop sign to manage traffic as a crossing guard during the next school year. It would be quite an honor for a ten-year-old like me but it's not going to happen no matter how responsible and mature I am.

I shouldn't have been surprised about the move since there had been a lot of whispered conversations between my mother and my grandmother in the weeks ahead of it. Grandma comes to visit every week, usually driving from St. Joseph to Kansas City on Thursdays in her bulbous old Pontiac, then turning around and heading back north before suppertime. We always eat better the night she comes, hamburger or cube steak with potatoes and milk gravy instead of our usual navy beans or short ribs with sauerkraut, dishes that can be stretched over several meals. Grandma always brings treats, too; Hershey bars, Planter's peanuts, Guy's potato chips and other dime snacks from behind the bar in the tavern. Mostly, though, she brings Mom solace and encouragement.

She needs some. Mom is trying to raise a ten-year-old, a five-year-old, and a toddler just recovering from an illness that left him brain-damaged with the motor skills of a newborn. Walt, father of the two younger boys, my half-brothers, sometimes works and sometimes doesn't—mostly doesn't—but always has time for a beer with the boys and especially for one with any girls that happen along during his travels. To keep ends together and pay the rent on our three-room shotgun apartment, Mom takes in ironing from the neighbors. That is about the only thing she can do with three kids at home and no such thing as child care available. Not that she could get a job that paid much if she were able to work outside the home anyway. Mom had dropped out of school at sixteen, waited tables in the tavern for a couple of years, married and became pregnant with me, and was a divorced single mother by the time she was twenty. Her job skills are severely limited, to say the least. When she finally gives up on Walt, her only option was to move back to St. Joseph where I was born.

The town snuggles alongside the levees that tame the Missouri River. It spreads inland across the hills and flats of neighborhoods that replaced the farms that themselves replaced woods and prairies. The river sparkles blue under the early spring sun, but turns a flat brown streaked with gray as the rains fill it up with the runoff from the surrounding fields and factories. You know just by looking at the water as it rolls heavily between the levees that it flows over a river bottom greasy and mucked up.

St. Joseph itself is just like the river. Lewis and Clark stopped there, but they didn't stay long. A few decades after they left, according to popular mythology, the town became a bustling mercantile center where the Old West met the gods of commerce. In truth, the town's sweet history had some rancid footnotes. The Pony Express, for example, started in St. Joseph. It ended there, too, bankrupt a year after the first intrepid rider floated across the river on the ferry and dashed away into the sunset toward Sacramento. The legendary Jesse James got himself shot dead in his house at Thirteenth and Olive Streets in St. Joseph, but not in a heroic gunfight with eager law officers. No, the sniveling Bob Ford shot him in the back of the head to collect some blood money. It seems like the town's history is all that way. Lots of good beginnings that ended sour.

Even the fable of why St. Joseph faded while nearby Kansas City prospered reads like a morality tale. At one time in the early years, Kansas City wasn't much more than a wide place in the muddy road just fifty miles south of St. Joseph. In the early years, the two towns competed for the business of outfitting wagon-trains for land-hungry settlers coming from the East, selling them wagons and the pots and pans and barrels of flour and all the other profitable provender that the pioneers needed to build a civilization in the West. The settlers, in turn, filled the bank accounts of the sturdy merchants of the two towns. St. Joseph got more than its share. The difference between the two, though, and what happened to make Kansas City leap ahead, was the way they each greeted the arrival of the railroad. Kansas City jumped at the chance to build a bridge across the Missouri River and got real friendly with the railroad companies. The rich burghers of St. Joseph's mercantile establishment, though, liked the status quo just fine. They much preferred the rails to end at the river's edge, where they could sell goods by the wagon load to the settlers when they were forced to de-train. Besides, the railroads had the unmitigated gall to expect the town to build the bridge for them! Where was the profit in that? You can see what happened. There are probably still warehouses in St. Joseph with back rooms full of wagon harnesses and buggy whips.

The town also had a long, shameful history of race hatred dating to its history as part of a slave state admitted to the Union under the terms of the Missouri Compromise. St. Joseph was a hotbed of pro-slavery raiders who repeatedly rode into neighboring Kansas in the decade before the Civil War in an attempt to keep that state from prohibiting slavery. Abraham Lincoln wisely chose not to campaign in the town when he first ran for president.

Turn a few more yellowed pages of the town history and you learn that St. Joseph also "hanged a colored man" one time. But that wasn't in the mists of history; it happened in 1931, when the Civil War was long over and Bloody Kansas across the river was nothing more than the ill-remembered ramblings of a couple of drunks down on Fourth Street who repeated stories they had heard from their grandfathers. St. Joseph should have been more civilized and humane twenty years before I was born in the twentieth century, but it wasn't.

A mere thirty years after the lynching, we move to St. Joseph. We live in the basement of the Ko-Z-Inn, the neighborhood tavern my grandmother owns, in an apartment of sorts that hasn't been used for anything except storage for many years. The front door is below street level and opens onto a patch of dirt at the front of some concrete stairs leading up to the sidewalk. Next to the stairs is a ramp used by deliverymen bringing cases of beer for storage in the basement room next to the apartment.

The front room of the space where we live holds a sofa and chair and a small TV set that receives exactly one channel on its rabbit ears antenna. The only window is the one in the front door, so the room is always dark. Looking back, every place we ever lived was dark. There were no sun-filled rooms cheery with ruffled curtains on mullioned windows because there were only one or two windows in the apartments, usually one in the front and one in the back. Other buildings always crowded the sides of ours. The Ko-Z-Inn squats on top of our cellar apartment. Oddly enough, even when Mom marries Lou and we move into a real house where I actually have my own room, it ends up being the only one in the house without a window. Maybe that's why I spend as much time outdoors as I can.

Once we settle, Mom finds some bunk beds at the second hand store and sets them up for Wayne and me so we can have a room of sorts in the passageway between the bathroom for the apartment and the room where the compressors run to chill the beer coolers for the tavern upstairs. Our beds are opposite some open-backed wooden stairs that climb to a trapdoor in the tavern floor, our ceiling. The door is thick and heavy and I can barely push it open. Every time I do, I imagine it falling back to crush my head. I would fall, I know, and tumble down the wooden stairs. I would probably break an arm or leg in the process and lay twisted on the dirt floor at the bottom of the stairs until I die in the dark.

Danger lurks in the compressor room, too, a place we aren't allowed to enter. The compressors have whirling wheels and belts that would slice off a careless finger without a hitch. Their motors chug and rumble all the time behind a thick wooden door that is locked, although I know how to open it. I don't like it in there. It is dark even when you pull the string for the light bulb in the ceiling. The dirt floor is damp and critters scurry around on it, always just out of sight. If you touch anything, your hand comes back grimy and greasy. Wayne won't even go near the door to that room, but I go in just to show him I am not afraid. "There's bugs in there!" he exclaims with wide, popping eyes. But his fear is okay. He is a little kid—five years younger than me—and as a big brother I am required to act brave in front of him.

Another locked door near our room secures an old workshop full of rusty hand tools our great-grandfather "borrowed" from the Missouri Pacific Railroad when he worked there. I am allowed to play with the clutter in the room. I get a couple of old ball peen hammers and a brace with some dull bits, but there's not much else good. I find a box of pencils and a stipple-covered account book I can draw in, but that's all. I am ten and the crusty wrenches and frozen calipers are of no use to me. Wayne is frightened of that room, too, and sidles along the opposite side of the passage when he needs to get by it to go upstairs. I understand.

I am too old to be much of a friend to Wayne. The five-year age difference will shape our relationship throughout our lives. I will always be there for him, but not as a friend or confidant. We will stick together because we have to. He will grow to be a solid, good-hearted man. He will make some bad decisions—don't we all?—but he will be a good father to his two daughters and a very good son to our mother.

The back room is where Mom sleeps with my brother Ken, a disabled toddler. There is a tiny kitchen off Mom's room that has a back door opening outside onto another patch of dirt. To get to Mom's room from the front room, you go past the bathroom, which has only a toilet and a sink, no bath tub or shower. The cellar doesn't have a hot water heater, but boys are dirty creatures, especially those who live in a hole in the ground like we do. Mom can bathe Ken in the kitchen sink, but for Wayne and me and herself, she resorts to a galvanized wash tub on the packed earth floor at the end of the passage where Wayne and I sleep. Like some kind of pioneer woman, she heats water on the kitchen stove and carries it in a bucket to the tub, which is just barely large enough for me to sit in with my knees drawn up to my chin. Wayne always goes first so Mom can wash him. I can take care of myself and the privacy is appreciated, but by the time I get to use the tub the water is tepid and cloudy and the bottom of the tub is gritty on my bare butt.

~~§~~

We live in a lightless cave and when you live in a cave, you expect there to be monsters. Mom leaves the bathroom light on at night, otherwise Wayne is too scared to go to sleep. The bathroom with its toilet and tiny sink has two doors, one to the passageway that serves as our bedroom, the other to the apartment with its cramped, lightless living room, utility kitchen, and Mom's bedroom in the back.

I have a little table tucked under the stairs opposite our beds where I can build model cars and planes and where I keep my library books and a cigar box with my stamp collection. Wayne sleeps in the bottom bunk and I on the top. I can reach the string to the ceiling light from my bed. Our floor is packed earth covered by a piece of loose linoleum and some braided rugs so we won't track dirt onto our bed sheets.

In the middle of the night, Wayne screams. I sit up in bed.

"Get them off me!" he screeches. "David! David! Get them off me!" I am scared, confused, try to shake off my sleep as his shouts grow louder.

I reach out and pull the cord to turn on the bare bulb in the ceiling. I lean over from the upper bunk so I can see Wayne in the yellow light. He cowers in the corner of his bed below, his little hands slapping at his legs and belly.

"Get them off! Get them off!" he pleads. I don't see anything on him.

"What?" I shout. "What are they?"

"Bugs and snakes! Spiders!" His eyes are wide open but unseeing. He is trapped in a nightmare, unable to wake up. His arms flail about his body. I shiver at the sight of his contorted face and the otherness of his eyes. I am scared but I climb down anyway and get into his bed. I try to help him brush away the imaginary horrors.

"It's okay," I say. "I'm here."

"Get them! Oh, get them off," he whimpers. His skin is clammy, his face covered with sweat, his pajamas soaked and clinging. He has wet himself.

I realize he is sick and run to get Mom. She comes to his bed and soothes him until he awakens.

"He's okay," she tells me. "He has a fever and it gave him a bad dream." She brings buckets of water from the kitchen and fills the wash tub. She strips off his pajamas and lays him in it. The water cools and calms him. She takes him back to her room to finish the night and I climb back into my bed. My mind can't erase the image of Wayne quivering in the corner of his bunk, eyes wide and seeing things only he can see. When morning comes, I am still awake.

Most nights, once we are in our room, I don't hear much from the rest of the apartment. The TV only gets one channel and its picture is fuzzy so Mom doesn't watch it much. She listens to the radio in her room sometimes or goes upstairs to talk to Grandma in her room next to the tavern. Sometimes I hear Mom come down the wooden stairs but most nights I sleep as she tiptoes past our beds.

Tonight, I awaken to something nudging the edge of my consciousness. I lay in bed, listen hard, and try to understand what is wrong. There are voices somewhere in the apartment saying things I can't make out. The words are angry, though, and when the front door crashes open, I jump out of bed.

"Mom!" I call through the bathroom.

"Go back to bed, David," she shouts. "It's all right." But it's not all right. There is anger in her voice.

"See! You woke them up," she hisses. "Get out! The judge said you can't come here."

"The hell with that," a man answers. "I'm not leaving until I get what's mine." It is Walt, I realize. It's the first time my stepfather has been around since we left him. Suddenly, I don't want to be in the dark. I pull the light cord and see Wayne sitting up in bed, rubbing his eyes.

"They aren't yours," Mom says. Someone stomps across the living room. "Get your hands off me!" she cries.

"Mom!" I yell as the scuffling comes closer. Just as I start through the connecting bathroom, they burst through the opposite door. Mom tries to hold him off but he pushes her through the doorway. I back out of the way as they bump past the toilet and the sink and into our room. He pins her against the wall next to our bed, panting and ranting about something he says is his. It takes a minute, but from what I finally understand from his ravings, Walt wants a handful of old postage stamps he claimed I stole from him. But they weren't his, they were mine. His mother had given me some old envelopes she had saved from before the war. I soaked the stamps off to add them to the collection I kept in a cigar box. When she gave them to me, he told me they were worthless, which they are. Now his greedy beer-soaked brain decided they are rare and valuable and he wants them.

I pick up the cigar box full of stamps on my desk, but drop it when Mom yells, "David! Go call the police!"

I run up the stairs, the wood biting my bare feet. I push against the heavy door in the ceiling with all my might and my knees quiver under its weight. I am petrified the thick cellar door is going to fall on my head. I have to do it, have to use all the strength in my skinny arms, have to get through that door to get to the telephone. Mom cries out from below, so I swallow my fear and shove.

The door slips against my shoulder as I get it open, but I don't let it fall. I push it up and latch it to the wall so it will stay open.

"Where are they?" Walt demands. I can't see him, but I know he is still pushing her against the wall below.

"I don't know," Mom says. Her voice sounds pinched. I think he is strangling her.

I run through the dark tavern to the cash register behind the bar. I push the "No Sale" lever and grab a quarter marked with red paint out of the drawer. The only phone we have is the pay phone in the tavern. When the phone company empties it, they give the red quarters back to Grandma.

I dial the number for the police listed on the front of the phone. I give them the address and tell them Walt is trying to kill my mom. I have to repeat it twice, but they finally understand me.

"The cops are coming!" I shout. I run back to the cellar door and down the stairs. As I get to the bottom, he steps away from her.

"Now you better get out!" Mom snarls in his face.

He turns and spots my cubby under the stairs. He grabs the cigar box with my sad little stamp collection. Mom smacks it out of his hands and stamps scatter everywhere. A siren sounds in the distance. Walt turns and runs. I follow him through the apartment and slam the front door behind him.

When I come back, Mom is sitting on Wayne's bunk, rocking him against her body. There are red marks on her arms. She is laughing and crying at the same time.

"He wanted those stupid stamps," she says.

I don't tell her they are worthless. Wayne whimpers softly in her arms while I gather the stamps off the floor. I am ten years old and I don't know what to say to the cops when they knock on the door.

Mom, 1951

Tooth Fairy Daddy

I drew a picture of my father; he could not see.

All around him in the blackness there were demons.

I danced and sang dirges while

tirades flowed from his lips and he cried he could not be with me.

So I wanted.

I drew the picture but I didn't know his secret thoughts

or anything about him except he pushed a broom

somewhere and he was gone.

He pulled my tooth once, in his overalls in the principal's office. Pop!

It was gone.

His chambray shirt was starched and neat,

the sleeves buttoned, and the collar buttoned,

and no patches anywhere.

He might have smiled or grunted.

I put the tissue with my tooth in the pocket

of my rayon shirt that screamed red and black slashes on white.

How long? How many?

More and more flew around his head,

wings flitter-flapping, tails snapping, beaks clicking and eyes popping.

Squeaks and squeals and screeches from some.

Others sang wash-day songs and sucked their teeth.

We danced and dirged.

"Are you okay now?"

"Sure. Thanks. Do you live here?"

"No, I work here just to see you."

He disappeared in the crowded hall. Big kids shoved to class.

Bells rang; papers rustled; the buzz of the lights blanked out the songs.

I didn't see him go.

I knew where he was, though: down

in the basement deeper underneath,

tending the iron boiler with his talented hands.

Bright, bright light bulbs. Hard shadows everywhere.

Me nowhere. Him down

there with a red handkerchief in the pocket of his overalls like a farmer.

The picture didn't have a sky.

A lost boy goes behind Safeway to play among the splintered boxes

and eat wild peaches.

You hear the freezer engines humming and

smell milk soured on the asphalt

but far enough away it gets better and dusty in the tall, dry weeds.

The peach tree is wild but

was there a house there one long time ago? Maybe.

He would have been, too, but, you know.

I went home to draw some pictures of stick people and forgot.

The tissue melted in the wash with my tooth.

He melted, too,

I guess, into the sky that wasn't there or

into the boiler or into the milk on the asphalt behind Safeway.

I sang and sang, but he never came back.

Barbara at KO-Z-INN, c 1949

Mom
And
Family

Sarah Welch (my great-great-grandmother)
with Barbara on her lap.
(clockwise from left), Margie, Frances, Cecile,
Josie, Cecile Alice, 1932

Family

Historically, women are the most steadfast characters in my family saga. There are plenty of men in the story, but few of them stuck around very long. When you look into my not-distant past, you find women with multiple spouses and offspring of various parentages, but few men except one or two who became legends of a sort in the family canon.

We can dispense quickly with the family history on the Donelson side, mainly because I don't know much about it. Jeremy did some online genealogical research when Steve was born and came up with tenuous lineage to the Irish province of Ulster, which possibly confirms the family claim of Scots-Irish roots, but that's about all I know about any generations before my grandparents on my father's side.

Mom always said Jack's parents looked down on her, which I suppose could have been the case, but I don't think they were anything like the elite nabobs such a remark implies. Carl Donelson, my grandfather, made signs for taverns in the advertising department of the Goetz brewery. His sons, Jack and Billy, worked in the brewery, too, and both also finished high school. Their sister, Nancy, was a pretty and popular cheerleader. My grandmother Donelson, Goldie, kept a neat house, tended a garden, and herded everybody to the Wyatt Park Baptist Church every Sunday. To be fair, if she had an unfavorable opinion of my mom or her family, she never voiced it within my hearing.

While the Donelsons were a church-going and seldom-divorced clan, the Russells and McConnells had more romantic entanglements than a room full of horny bunnies.

Mom's family on her mother's side, the McConnells, can trace its beginnings in America to Pieter de Coninck II (who changed his name to Peter King II) and his wife Anna (nee Calet), who emigrated to New Amsterdam (New York) from Flanders in 1679. Peter King II was a direct descendant of Pieter de Coninck, a commoner who led a series of uprisings against the French rulers of Bruges, his hometown, in 1302. A highlight of the rebellion was the "Matins of Bruges" which occurred at sunrise on May 18 when de Coninck led his band of commoners against their burgher masters, slaughtering as many as 4,000 Frenchmen and their supporters. According to The Golden Spurs of Kortrijk: How the Knights of France Fell to the Foot Soldiers of Flanders in 1302 by Randall Fegley (McFarland 2002), "...it was Pieter de Coninck, a poor weaver from Bruges...,whose intelligence and oratorical talents motivated listeners to follow him in an unprecedented series of uprisings. Though short in stature, he was clearly the commoners' champion...." My distant ancestor's actions ultimately led to the Battle of the Golden Spurs, which ended French domination of Flanders. De Coninck was knighted for his accomplishments and became an alderman, but that didn't make him any less a rebel. In 1309 he led another uprising in Bruges, this one against the peace treaty of Athis-sur-Orge, which he opposed since he believed it was bad for Flanders. In 1321 he rebelled yet again but was punished for it by having his possessions confiscated and sold. From what I know about him, I like this guy.

Ernest McConnell, my great-grandfather, was a descendant of de Coninck. He farmed with his wife, Josie (nee Welch), in Little River, Kansas, before he went to work for the Missouri Pacific railroad. The pair moved around quite a bit over the years. They lived in Falls City and Surprise, Nebraska, as well as other railroad towns where Josie ran boarding houses for railroad men (as had her mother in York, Nebraska) while Ernest kept payroll records for the railroad. Josie was a good cook and a very good baker, according to Mom, who often used some of the recipes Josie handed down to her. Many of them weren't original, though. Josie copied down more than a few of them listening to radio programs like Kitchen Klatter airing from Shenandoah, Iowa. Josie and Ernest loved corn on the cob, but the household rule was you had to eat the corn within a half hour of picking it.

Ernest was a little man, but he could reputedly bring a mule to its knees with a hard rap on its nose with the first knuckle of his right hand. He was an energetic man, too, who never walked when he could trot from task to task. True to his upbringing on a farm, he always planted big gardens. Josie spent her summers canning what they grew and Ernest brought 100-pound bags of potatoes to his daughters when they married and moved out of the family home.

If Josie had a complaint, it was that Ernest believed he needed sex (and insisted on it) every three days regardless of her thoughts on the matter. Despite all the lovemaking, the pair only had two children. Their first, my grandmother, was named Cecile (pronounced "Cecil" like the man's name) who worked the farm in rolled up overalls right alongside her father, driving a mule team and doing anything else a man could do. Their younger daughter, Frances, was small and dainty and given to fits of fainting. My mother is said to resemble her although I've never known Mom to faint.

Cecile married three men in quick succession. She was 17 and living in Kansas on her parents' farm when she married the first time. The groom was

41

A. J. McCreary, a railroad engineer, and the marriage lasted four short years, which was long enough for her to bear two daughters, Frances Fern and Cecile Alice. Cecile divorced McCreary in 1924 and married Howard Allen the next year. That pairing lasted about a year. Then Bill Russell came into her life.

Bill Russell, my grandfather, is a legendary character in the family chronicle. My smile evokes memories of his, according to my mother. She says it's quick and sincere and starts in the eyes, just like his. I like to think I inherited more than just his smile, though. He played the piano and the fiddle, guitar, and banjo—anything with strings—but never learned to read music. He was a carpenter who could turn a few boards into a table or a doll house or a picket fence. I treasure a cello he crafted out of the headboard of an old bed. He wasn't afraid to try anything, and if he failed at it, he just smiled and moved on to something else that caught his fancy. He had many regrets but didn't dwell on any of them. I don't know if I inherited some of that from him or if I just picked it up from hearing the stories, but I am glad I have his general outlook on life. The only failure that matters is failing to try.

When he was eleven, Bill ran away from home in Broken Bow, Nebraska, and hopped a passing freight train. His mother, Edith, was fifteen when he was born and was said to have had many lovers, some of them bearing gratuities. She married a few and didn't marry others and bore several children along the way. One of the men, perhaps a stepfather, beat Bill one time too many, so the youngster hit the road leaving his brothers and sisters behind.

Somewhere early in his travels, Bill met Mr. and Mrs. Reno. They were vaudevillians, he a magician, she a contortionist. Bill's part in their act was to play "Turkey in the Straw" on a fiddle while the Reno's little bulldog, Major, danced in circles on his hind legs. The Renos toured the country and Bill grew up to be a musician.

Bill met Cecile in Omaha. At the time, Josie had a boardinghouse and Ernest worked in the railroad office. The sequence of events is a bit confused, but Josie and Ernest adopted Cecile's two girls from her first marriage, their grandchildren Frances Fern and Cecile Alice, sometime before her marriage to Bill in 1927. One version of the story said cruelly that Bill wouldn't marry Cecile if the children came with her, although that's almost certainly not true since he always accepted the girls and introduced them as his daughters later in their lives. More likely, it happened before Bill came along. Cecile would have been struggling with the financial travails of a 20-something divorcee with two small children and few resources beyond what her parents could provide. She had few skills other than the ability to push a plow behind a mule. Regardless of the reasons, Cecile and her parents made a tough decision.

After they married, Bill and Cecile had two daughters of their own, Margie, sarcastically nicknamed the "golden child" by her sisters, and then Barbara, my mother. Bill played his fiddle for dances and house parties and broke into radio at KFAB in Omaha. The medium was in its infancy but growing rapidly and Bill dragged his little family around behind him when he went to work at pioneering stations in Iowa, Missouri, Kansas, and even as far away as Detroit. Family lore has it that Bill got lost in the big city when he drove the family to Michigan. When some wiseacre spotted the Iowa plates on the car and yelled for him to get back to the farm where he belonged, Bill hollered back that he gladly would if he could find it! Bill hooked up with Lawrence Welk in Yankton, South Dakota, and Gene Autry somewhere else along the way, and played in their bands, although he didn't stay with either one. Finally Cecile had enough of life on the road and got a boardinghouse of her own in St. Joseph. She set her mind to settling Bill down to a semi-normal life. Mom was six years old at the time.

In St. Joseph, Bill played on KFEQ radio (a station where I worked 35 years later) as well as at dances around the area. His stage name was "Bunkhouse" Bill and he played with a string band known as the "Bunkhouse Boys."

Bill had a little workshop in a shed behind the boarding house where he repaired instruments for both fellow musicians and the local music store downtown, the Eshelman Music House. I had a brief business relationship with Eshelman's, too, although it ended on a sour note. I was browsing in the store one day not long after Eileen and I married and I overheard one of the salesmen tell a customer that the store couldn't provide guitar lessons for her daughter because their teacher had recently moved out of town. I promptly volunteered my services and a deal was struck after I briefly demonstrated my ability on the guitar the customer was buying. A lesson was set for the next day. The mother asked if her daughter would need a lesson book. Ever the salesman, I grabbed one off a nearby shelf and she bought it without question. Unfortunately, I'd never seen a lesson book before since I was entirely self-taught and played by ear. Everything fell apart during the first lesson. I tried to teach my new student how to form a pump handle C chord but she demanded I show her how to play the notes in the first lesson in her new book. She became quite indignant when I spent ten minutes trying to figure out how to do that. Never having taken a lesson myself, I didn't have a clue. When she told Eshelman's I couldn't read music, my brief career as a music teacher at the store came to a Harold Hill end.

Cecile's plan to build a normal life for her family was easier said than achieved. She was a strong farm girl who had a business to run and a family to raise. Bill and his daughters may have been living a happy-go-lucky life, but Cecile certainly wasn't. She let him know it, too. Compounding the complications of Bill's irregular hours and catch-as-catch-can income were the lives of Cecile's boarders, most of whom were also musicians. Chaos generally ruled the day in the boarding house despite her best efforts to maintain order.

Meanwhile, Frances Fern and Cecile Alice were growing up with their grandparents in Falls City, Nebraska. Ernest and Josie took the two girls around the country by taking advantage of his railroad employee's pass. They went as far as New York City, eating bread-and-butter sandwiches and fried chicken Josie packed to take along. Frances Fern graduated from high school in 1939, Cecile Alice in 1941. They spent summers with Bill and Cecile and the two little girls, although Cecile Alice usually got homesick for her grandmother and went back to Falls City after a couple of weeks in St. Joseph.

A 1945 family tragedy in far-off California brought matters to a complicated head. Bill's half-sister, Alma, was living in Compton with another sister, Myrtle, who owned a tavern, and their mother, Edith. A careless driver ran down and killed Alma's two-year-old son, sending her deep into a depression that drew Bill to California to help her. His announced plan was to bring her back to St. Joseph to recuperate, but she swallowed a fatal dose of rat poison before that could happen.

We'll never know for sure why, but Bill never came back. Someone in that branch of the family had staked a claim under the Homestead Act to some property with a less-than-successful gold mine in Perris, California. Bill, Myrtle, and their mother moved there and assumed the claim. Cecile made the trek to California to bring Bill back, but couldn't persuade him. They never divorced but it was the end of their marriage.

~~∫~~

I'm getting a bit ahead of the timeline, but Mom's three sisters played supporting roles in my life, especially Frances Fern, my Aunt Franny. She was particularly close to Mom. She also had a rough-and-tumble romantic life that included six husbands and one guy who thought he was going to be number seven. Mom's tally of Franny's marriages was a little vague but had just enough telling detail to have the ring of truth. "After she graduated from high school," Mom said, "she married her high school sweetheart, Don Fenton, but that didn't last. Then she joined the WACS during the war to get away from St. Joe but they posted her right back to Rosecrans Field after training in Des Moines. When she got out, she married two other guys I can't remember, then she met Ray Stock and married him in 1946. I had told her about the handsome new boarder we had. It was Ray, hubba hubba!" If my math is correct, Franny married four times in the seven years after she got her high school diploma—and a year and a half of that time was spent in the army.

Ray and Franny were married for thirty years, though, and adopted two kids along the way. When Mom and Jack split up, I was barely a toddler and she and I lived with them. Later, Aunt Franny saved my brother Ken's life.

After their kids grew up and moved away, Franny and Ray moved to California to live with Bill and his sister Myrtle. Ray died in 1977. Bunkhouse Bill passed away in 1982 and his sister, Myrtle, a couple of years later. Franny showed up at Mom's house later that year with several thousand dollars in cash for Mom. When asked where she got it, she explained that the beneficiary of Myrtle's original will was some animal shelter, which Franny thought wasn't fair since she had cared for the woman for years while the animals in the shelter hadn't done a damn thing for her. In the interests of justice, Franny "found" another will that rectified that egregious error. This cash was Mom's share since Bill was her natural father and his interest in the Perris property had gone to Myrtle. It was only fair.

46

After Franny left the state of California for Florida, she married a Mexican gentleman who demanded sex three times every day, at least according to what she told my mother. Worn out, she soon divorced him and married a less-demanding guy for a while. She finally wrapped up her romantic career cohabitating in Tampa with a garrulous fellow named Bob. Mom and I met Bob when we visited Franny in the trailer park where they lived. Franny suffered from a degenerative bone disease in her spine and was legally blind from macular degeneration. It was clear to us that Bob was living off her meager old age benefits and waiting for her to die so he could get her trailer. Not long after we visited, Franny fooled everybody by kicking Bob out. She sold the trailer and moved in with her daughter in Tennessee, where she finally stopped getting married and died five years later.

Going back in time to pick up another thread of the story, her sister Cecile Alice married after the war and moved to Florida where she opened an antique store with her husband, Alex. She gave birth to my cousin Tom, then divorced his father. She soon married my uncle Hank, whose first wife had died and left him with a son, Henry. Hank was a flyer at McGill Air Force Base in Tampa. My cousin Keith was born a few days after me in 1951.

In 1948, my grandmother gave up on Bill, sold the boarding house and bought the Ko-Z-Inn, a neighborhood tavern on the corner of 22nd Street and Mitchell Avenue. The place had a grill and steam table, a long wooden bar and a handful of plywood booths along one wall. It also had a license to sell 3.2 % beer, a supposedly non-intoxicating holdover from the Volstead Act that made the Ko-Z-Inn one of only a couple of places in town that could serve beer on Sundays. The weekday lunch crowd came from the Big Chief tablet factory a few blocks away as well as dozens of small shops in the neighborhood. There wasn't much dinner business, but the bar was active when the shifts changed.

Mom was sixteen when she moved to the rooms behind the tavern with her mother and older sister Margie. Margie could joke and carry on with the customers, but Mom was too embarrassed to do anything other than take their quarters and give them a beer. She did, however, meet Jack there. Their marriage didn't last long much longer than my gestation and she went back to work in the tavern when they divorced. According to Mom, I learned to walk in the Ko-Z-Inn by toddling from bar stool to bar stool. She frequently propped me up in an empty beer case on the end of the bar where the patrons got a kick out of feeding me saltines. This may not have met the Donelson family's standards.

Mom met her other two husbands in the tavern, too. She married Walt in 1953 against everyone's advice and the three of us moved to Kansas City, where my two other half-brothers, Wayne and Ken, were born. After that unhappy marriage ended, the four of us moved back to the tavern, where she met Lou.

Six months after I was born in 1951, my great-grandmother, Josie McConnell, passed away. Ernest moved into a room in the tavern where his daughter Cecile could take care of him, which is why there was no room for Mom and me when she split up with Jack. Ernest was 70 at the time and long retired from the railroad. It was his collection of tools and office supplies I found in a dirt-floored room in the basement of the tavern. I still have a few of the odds and ends.

Even in his 70s, Ernest was a randy old goat. Despite his daughter's vocal disapproval, he often slipped out of his room and caught a bus downtown to look for love in all the wrong places, as the song goes. Cecile finally went totally berserk when, after disappearing one night, he got off the bus in the front of the tavern the next morning holding hands with a younger and much disheveled woman. The pair tried to slip into his room unnoticed, but Cecile met them at the door. She demanded to know who he thought he was bringing into her house, so Ernest announced grandly that the woman was going to be his new wife. Cecile grabbed a handy broom and brandished it in the woman's face. "Not here, she's not!" she exclaimed. The woman didn't stick around to discuss the matter. Not long afterward, Ernest was sent to live with his granddaughter and adopted daughter, Franny, in Gallatin, Missouri.

Franny says she brought him home on the bus as he struggled and protested to the other passengers that he was being kidnapped. When she got him to her house, the first place she took him was to the bathroom for some much needed ablutions. She drew a bath and sent him in to use it, but he faked it behind closed doors and went to bed. The next night, Franny waited until she heard him get undressed in the bathroom, then barged in and confiscated his cringe-inducing underwear before scrubbing him down herself. The next day, he wandered around town telling anyone who would listen that she had used a household scrub brush on him. Ernest may have been cleaner, but he wasn't any tamer. Not wanting to lock him in his bedroom, Franny balanced an empty can on his doorknob to serve as an alarm, a measure she had to take after he wandered away one too many times in the middle of the night, naked except for his hat.

In the woodshop, 2013

Woodworking

Shaved wood curls on the floor

Tawny and crushed,

Lost underfoot

But redolent of tree life eternal.

Sun slants through cobwebbed windows

Sawdust clings to air.

Squeeze clamp, check for square, nudge

Golden glue drops on the floor

Wait for morning

Kick dry leaves from the door.

But before all that,

Build patience with patience

Conceive, think through joints, pressure points, stresses.

Square the stock, measure, measure, cut.

Fit and try.

Glue.

Never perfect but always strong.

Barbara Lea Russell, May 24, 1934

Tales From Barbara

In 1995, I gave Mom a little book called "Share Your Life with Me." It had 365 blank pages with leading questions about her life that she was to answer. She completed it and sent it back on my birthday with this note:

Dear David,

I'm not very proud of this book but I think faster than I can write & really get a little messy with my writing & I'm sure there is some misspelled words. (sic) I skipped the limerick part, not very good at rhymes. It was fun filling out your book, but I'm afraid it is rather boring reading. Your mother wasn't a very exciting person, dear. I made a lot of mistakes in my life but the good things were my three sons! So I guess it wasn't a complete flop. Have a wonderful birthday!

Love,

Mom

An edited summary of Mom's recollections. . . .

I was born on April 16, 1932, at home in Omaha, Nebraska. Attending was Dr. Rance, my dad, my sister Margie, and my grandma and grandpa.

Dad called me his "little Dutchman" because of the way I talked. Grandma called me her "little funny face." My third grade teacher called me her "little ray of sunshine." Dad called Cecile his "little Indian" and Frances was "Franny Fern." I called Margie "Marnie" and we all called Franny "Sarge" because she was good at giving orders.

My grandpa, Ernest, was always busy. One time, I was playing fox and crow, hopping around in the yard, while Grandpa was nailing upholstery on a chair. When Grandma told him he wasn't getting the lines straight, he said, "I could, if that damned kid would quit hopping in circles!"

Grandpa always put out enough garden for an army. I remember Grandma worked so hard trying to can and preserve everything. She always looked so stern, but was a very loving Grandma. I used to have to visit them in Falls City because I would get homesick for her. Her house in Surprise, Nebraska, had an outhouse and I hated to go out there because of the bees and because I was scared I would fall in the hole. Grandma always went with me.

My aunt Frances and her husband Earl had two daughters. Nina was four years younger than me and she ran at me one time and bit me in the stomach.

We lived in Topeka when I was three or four and Dad always had to play for the state fair. There were a lot of Indians from the reservations there and I was scared to death of them.

Dad made Margie and me a table, two chairs, and a cabinet for Christmas when I was six. I discovered there was no Santa that year when I saw Mom and him putting them under the tree. The furniture was bright red with black trimmings. There were animals on each corner of the table. We loved to play paper dolls, who of course were always movie stars. We also played jacks and jump rope. I had a little dog named "Button," a terrier. She used to lay in the shade when Nancy and I would sit in our play furniture that Dad made for us. When she got sick, Dad had to put Button down with his rifle.

Dad was a hard punisher but did it very seldom. Mom was worse since she always gave a lecture for thirty minutes or so! One time, Margie told on Marilyn and me for hiding cigarettes in Marilyn's bike compartment and we got a good scolding. I only got one spanking from Dad. Margie and I were supposed to be in bed, but there was a full moon and I took up dancing the hula in front of the screen door. He was trying to sleep and keep telling us to quiet down, but, like girls do, we got the giggles and couldn't stop. I sobered right up after he paddled my behind.

We had a boarding house from the time I was six until I turned sixteen. There was always something going on and we had a lot of good times there. If we had a new roomer the others always made him or her welcome by putting oatmeal in their bed or short-sheeting them. With a house full of musician roomers, there was always a party. We had a lot of fun but very little privacy.

I recall Dad getting choked on a donut—he always dunked them in his Postem—and Mom and Franny hung his arms over the clothes line and pounded on his back until he could breathe. When he caught his breath, he just grinned and said he got choked on the hole in the donut.

There was no end to chores like washing dishes in the boarding house. Margie always seemed to have to go to the bathroom when it was time for drying them. Whenever Mom got mad about something she mopped the floors or changed the beds. We had very clean floors and neat beds.

My Dad was my only hero and I loved him dearly. He always told me, "Pretty is as pretty does." He could fix anything and he was always ready to play a game with us. He helped me very much with my music. He was a stickler for keeping perfect time and would keep it with his foot on the piano bench while I was playing. I loved to lean over Dad's back and put my hands on his while he played. Because of him, music meant a lot to me and if I had a small worry, I'd go play the piano.

I really don't have any talents except playing the piano, I guess. Back then, every couple had a love song and the roomers furnished me with the sheet music to play theirs for them. We saw a lot of roomers go away to war and it was very sad. Many of them wrote to us about how homesick they were.

We had a lot of KFEQ radio entertainers rooming with us and they had a lot of jam sessions. We loved to dance. It was hard not to dance when Dad played since he just had a lot of good rhythm to his music.

Dad had a small trailer that he hauled instruments in for the band. My friends and I used to hide in it to smoke when it was parked in the yard. A nosy neighbor told Mom that it was on fire one time, so that put an end to that. Dad played with a band at Lake Contrary. The pavilion there had the best dance floor in town. My friend Nancy and I rode under his bass fiddle in the back of the car many times. We got to go on the rides while he played for the dances. I liked the big dipper, the roller coaster, the figure eight, bumper cars, and shoot-the-chute boat rides.

I always wanted to be a housewife and mother when I grew up. I used to say I was going to have twelve children, but after three I changed that tune.

Jack used to come into the tavern with three other guys and I waited on them. Then we started dating. Our first date was New Year's Eve and we went to another couple's house and played cards. Jack was a little shy but nice. He had a very hearty laugh. We got married at Wyatt Park Baptist Church on August 1, 1950. I wore a very light blue dress and a navy pillbox hat with a veil. Dr. White performed the ceremony and Margie and Ray stood up for us. We both got the giggles when Jack couldn't get the ring on my finger. We didn't have any money so we didn't go on a honeymoon.

We lived at 2402 ½ Patee Street in an attic apartment with a small porch. There was a very small bedroom, kitchen, living room, and a bath. It was upstairs and very hot.

One time, Jack and I were fishing at Bee Creek near Dearborn with Margie and her husband, also named Jack. My Jack and I were out on a sandbar when we saw a bull about a quarter block away pawing his hoof and looking mean. I had on a red blouse and I was ready to strip it off but Jack talked me out of that idea and kept me calm until we were out of there.

Jack liked to play poker at the filling station on 22nd Street once in a while. He came home a couple of times with just two dollars from his paycheck. Thankfully, that finally wore off. We didn't have too many problems; just like most young couples we didn't have enough money. Our apartment was too hot and there was a little too much family in our lives.

My grandmother taught me to embroider and a woman who worked in the tavern taught me how to crochet. I was pregnant at the time and David got a lot of crocheted socks to wear.

On the day David was born, I was doing the laundry in our kitchen and it was very hot. I had a stomach ache and went to the hospital around 9:30 AM. The baby finally came about 4:30 PM. During his first month, he had the colic and it was very hard to get him to take a bottle.

As a baby, David rolled every place he wanted to go before he crawled. When he was six months old, he rolled off the bed at Franny's and Grandma thought his wailing was from a cat fight outside.

The advice I have for all my boys is to be happy and stay well! That's a mother's wish. You deserve to be happy because you have brought so much happiness to me.

1984

Music

Music has always been a part of me. Not just around me or in the background, but a near-physical part of my person. There's a song somewhere in my head all the time. Given my grandpa's and mom's talents, it's not surprising that music moves within me.

A persistent meme says that your musical tastes are formed in your teens. That was certainly true for me, although the corollary, that your favorite song for the rest of your life will be the chart topper of your sixteenth year, most probably wouldn't hold in my case. Oh, I liked popular music, but there's no way "To Sir With Love" is my favorite song of all time. I like it all right, because in my teens, as now, I preferred melodic ballads and complex harmonies over the bombastic, beat-driven tunes that fill play lists today. Still, there are plenty of other songs that stuck with me better than that one.

The music from my teens that meant the most to me were the songs I taught myself to play, originally on the tenor banjo and then on the guitar. The first ones were simple folk tunes—three or four chords and a melody you could hum or whistle. Then came Bob Dylan and Peter, Paul, and Mary with modern themes in the folk traditions—the music was still simple, but there was more variety to it. I discovered Josh White in a music book remainder rack and picked up some blues and traditional ballads from him. At one time, I had memorized hundreds of cover songs—Simon & Garfunkel, Kingston Trio, Gordon Lightfoot and the like—using my own arrangements and fingering. Now, I can remember the lyrics to no more than two dozen of them, although the melodies are all still there in my head.

That was always the strangest thing—I can hear and repeat a melody almost immediately, but lyrics are a chore. Today, I play from a homemade fake book with chord names and the words to a couple hundred songs because I can't remember the damn lyrics. I suppose if I sat down and forced myself to memorize them I could do it, but I'm not at all sure about that.

Fifty years ago, though, that's the way I taught myself to play. If I had never heard a song before, I could more or less decipher a melody on the treble clef, thanks to my Mom, and figure it out on the frets well enough to pick out a melody from sheet music if I didn't already know it. Then I used chord diagrams on the music to learn the changes. It was much easier for songs I had heard a few times since I could pretty much play the changes to match the melody line in my head. I sat in my room for two hours almost every day plugging away at "My Grandfather's Clock" and "Early Morning Rain" until I could play them without looking at the chord sheets. Do that long enough—and continually force yourself to tackle harder and harder material—and you can learn just about anything. That's how I learned to play.

The first instrument I played was a tenor banjo, which has four strings and is most often associated with ragtime and New Orleans jazz. It's versatile like a ukulele in that you can pick up simple fingerings on it pretty quickly and chord along with just about any kind of tune. The five-string, or plectrum, banjo is much harder to play at first, although like any stringed instrument, once you get the hang of the mechanics of it, it's not too bad. By the time I got a five-string (a bachelor party present, of all things), I was too deep into the guitar to really devote much time to it.

I took up the banjo originally because all the other kids were banging guitars and I wanted to be different. The banjo satisfied that need for a while, although I was ready to switch when Grandpa gave me my first guitar, an off-brand beater that I discarded when it stopped holding tune and I could afford my first real instrument. I was fifteen and it was a used Martin D-18. I still have it, even though it's in pretty bad shape. One of these days I might get it fixed up for old time's sake.

It wasn't long before I realized that if you can play one stringed instrument, you can play them all with some measure of success. I made an elementary balalaika just to see if I could and much later built a mandolin from a kit. Unfortunately, the joints in neither of them withstood the tests of time. Mom gave me an old fiddle of grandpa's and I managed to attached some geared tuners so I could play it after a fashion. Now, I entertain myself with a very fine classical guitar made by Masaki Sakurai.

Many other guys played in garage bands, but I performed in coffee houses either solo or with my classmate Joyce Perrin, an excellent finger-picker with a thin soprano voice who worshipped Joan Baez. There were two coffee houses where St. Joseph's small hippie community hung out. Both operated in the basement of local churches on Friday and Saturday nights as a way to keep the kids off the street. The first one that opened catered to the students at St. Joseph Junior College and called itself "Belly of the Whale." The college kids didn't want us high school kids around and continually kicked us out, so we found a place for ourselves in the basement of the First Presbyterian Church. We named it, of course, "Jonah's."

Jonah's was perfect. Lit by candles stuck in empty wine bottles on folding tables with permanently over-flowing ashtrays, it had a platform stage with a simple sound system and a couple of spot lights. You wouldn't want to see it in the daylight, but a bunch of us thought it was pretty cool. Joyce and I played there many times until, like Bob Dylan, she got infected by the rock and roll bug and went electric on me. Then I went solo.

I played house parties and a number of other places evenings after I got off work at the gas station. There were a handful of similar coffeehouses in Kansas City where I could pick up twenty bucks or so depending on the door that night. I also played a few ragtime banjo gigs at Shakey's Pizza Parlor, accompanying a piano player who performed a "sing along" repertoire of old timey songs with the lyrics flashed on the wall by a slide projector—a primitive karaoke system. The biggest venue I ever played was the Krug Park Bowl. The St. Joseph Pops Orchestra gave summer concerts there on Sunday nights and I performed during their intermission a couple of times. Got my picture in the newspaper and everything.

The non-verbal experience of letting tones and tempo fill your head completely is what makes music completely fulfilling. Music is also indescribable using words. As Marshall McLuhan pointed out, attaching verbal labels to anything changes it into the label, not the thing. In the case of music, which is an experience in time and tone; words are an obstruction. There are no lyrics for the Goldberg Variations, yet the work moves me in many ways. Music is a way of thinking, a path to awareness that follows a complex non-verbal language. Alfred Korzybski would identify music as a non-Aristotelian epistemology. When I play at my most intense concentration, I lose conscious contact with everything except the sound filling my head. I listen to instrumental music the same way. It is magic, a pure experience that exists in a separate dimension.

Bunkhouse Bill Russell

With Wayne, 1957

Childhood

The first place I remember living was in a shabby apartment over a corner grocery store in Kansas City with Mom and Walt. You had to climb a long flight of stairs to get to it. I wasn't much more than a toddler when we moved there—about four years old—and I got in big trouble when I visited a neighbor's yard. She was an elderly Dutch lady and I picked the blooms off a stand of tulips she had in front of her house. The old lady was apoplectic when she discovered the damage, but took one look at my cherubic face and gave me a big kiss instead of a beating. I suspect I gave her my toddler's version of my grandpa's smile, something that has stood me in good stead throughout my life.

I started school from that apartment—afternoon kindergarten, a big deal for a five-year-old. I couldn't wait to go. The school was a few blocks away and there was one very busy street I had to cross after waiting for the light. Mom walked me to school the first few days to make sure I knew the route and how to check the light before I crossed the street. Then she followed me for a couple of days while I demonstrated I could manage the trip myself until finally I was on my own.

One morning not long after I started walking myself to school, I disappeared from the apartment. When Mom realized I was gone, she went into a frenzy. She searched the grocery store below the apartment and roamed the neighborhood calling my name. Finally, the old Dutch lady heard her frantic calls and came out of her house to tell her she had seen me walking down the sidewalk a short time before. Mom took off in the direction she pointed and hadn't gone far when she realized where it led. She found me sitting in the empty kindergarten room patiently waiting for class to start. I told her I came early because I didn't want to be late.

I was the only white kid in my kindergarten class. Not that it bothered me. Kids are kids, and I was just glad to have some friends to play with. One of those friends was a little African-American girl. One day, Walt saw us walking down the sidewalk holding hands. That evening after he'd had a few beers with one of his buddies, he called me into the kitchen, bent me over his knee and paddled me good. I suppose the spanking hurt, but what I remember most vividly was his laughter as he did it. The punchline his buddy found so humorous was when he told me my girlfriend was a "pickaninny."

I was almost five when my brother Wayne was born. Mom soon tired of hauling him up and down the stairs to the apartment over the grocery store, so we moved to a bigger apartment on the first floor of a four-unit building in a different part of town. An old lady and her alcoholic husband lived upstairs and our friends the Simmons lived on the first floor on the other side of the building. They had two sons. Greg was a year older than me and Geoff was about Wayne's age. Greg and I roamed the neighborhood with a gang of other kids, mostly Irish and Italian. The black neighborhood we had left was a few blocks away on the other side of Independence Avenue. Greg's mother, Betty, was small and petite like Mom, and they were good friends until Greg drowned at a school picnic and the Simmons moved away.

As poor as we were, Mom saw to it that we had as normal a childhood as she could make happen. She signed me up for Cub Scouts and served as den mother herself. Walt got into the act, too, mostly so he could do the projects—build my Pinewood Derby racer and make my Indian costume—rather than go to work and earn a paycheck. Since I didn't know or care about his reasons at the time, it was all good to me.

The scouts had a baseball league, too, and I played shortstop on our pack's team. At the age of eight, I wasn't much of a fielder and a worse batter, but since Walt was the assistant manager, I played every game. I did manage to get on base with regularity, though. Walt taught me to put my weight on my back foot in the batter's box and stand with my front foot balanced on its toes so I couldn't duck when the pitcher threw inside. I don't remember ever getting a hit, but I recall many trips to first base rubbing my arm or thigh and holding back the tears.

I went to summer camp once. It was on a "scholarship" from the Salvation Army. We shopped in their second-hand store and one of their kind volunteers made the offer. The Army ran the camp and I've had a warm spot in my heart for the organization ever since. I was only there for a week, but I learned to swim and only cried for my Mom the first night. The counselors were kind and I don't recall any proselytizing beyond a lot of songs about Jesus sung around the campfire.

I may have spent only a week at camp, but I've spent a lifetime in libraries. My love for books started early. Mom read to me every night, cuddling me on her lap while she read and re-read from a dog-eared book of fairy tales she had found in the thrift shop. When we moved, a branch of the Kansas City Public Library became a favorite haunt. It was an imposing stone edifice, dark and cool inside. The library was a hike from our apartment, but I made it every week, at first with Mom and later by myself. You could check out four books at a time, which wasn't enough to satisfy me but the limit was probably for the best since if I had my way I would have escaped into a book every waking minute, never seeing the outdoors or running around the neighborhood with the gang.

I was a bright child and books made me brighter, laying the foundation for success in school and beyond. Many times, books have also been my sanctuary, which can be both good and bad. I wonder sometimes if I would have closer relationships with other people if I hadn't spent so much time with my nose in a book. It's too late to break the habit now, though—not that I want to.

When you are seven years old, you only have one key—but it's an important one. It's not the key for the apartment in Kansas City and certainly not the one that starts your stepdad's car, which would be ridiculous since you can't reach the pedals and see over the steering wheel at the same time anyway. You could steal his church key, but you better not. Stick with the one on the string around your neck, the only key that's truly yours, and the only one that matters to Jenny, the girl with the blonde ponytail who lives around the block. She has one just like it. A skate key.

Yours hangs heavy on cotton twine over your t-shirt against your bony chest, a hex wrench on one end where the string goes through and a square tube on the business end, the part you use to clamp the steel-wheeled skates to your shoes before you clamber down the steps to meet Jenny waiting below. Your skate-clad feet slide, push, slide, push, slide, push over the sidewalk, jumping curbs and skipping over cracks one skate at a time, swooping downhill like an eagle diving from the sky and laboring uphill, huffing and swinging your sweaty arms, never peeking at your flying feet, eyes scanning the concrete ahead for pot holes, driving your skates with the burning pistons of your thighs.

You start on Garner, the street where you live near the corner. You go left because that's downhill so you can get going pretty well, lean into the corner, and whip around left onto Askew. The sidewalk is flat but bumpy and you have to keep your eyes open when you get to the alley because it's full of gravel and busted concrete that snags your wheels. Your chest tightens at the alley, too, because that's where you saw the boys trying to stick a kitten's tail into the oily flame of a smudge pot left by a street crew last year when you were six and just learning to skate. You are glad Jenny didn't see that.

At Smart Avenue you turn left again, slower now because the long uphill stretch begins. The apartment houses are bigger here and Jenny lives in the middle of the block. She joins you as you pass her building and you lean into the job and push the heavy skates with choppy strides. You pump your arms for extra power. Jenny's longer legs carry her in front of you but that's okay because you like to watch her pony tail swing from side to side across her back.

Another left turn and you're on Bales. Catch your breath. Let the pounding in your temples slow. This sidewalk is new and smooth so your skates slide easily down the slight slope back to Garner. One more turn and it's race time down the hill in the stretch to home.

You go around the block a hundred times or maybe a thousand. You skate with Jenny until it's dark and the bumps and cracks are hard to see and your steel skates grind over the concrete and leave a trail of sparks like Buck Rogers' rocket ship. You take her sweaty hand and she squeezes yours back.

~~§~~

Other times, afoot and alone, you explore the alley that runs from Smart Avenue almost through to Bales parallel to Garner. It passes the concrete pad behind your apartment building. The pad serves as the floor for wooden storage sheds and the roof for dirt-floored one-car garages beneath it at alley level. You want to see something nasty, all you have to do is go down the cracked concrete steps from the yard to the alley and look around. The alley will show it to you if you look—and you don't have to look very hard. The alley is wicked.

People tell you to stay out of the alley because there's evil stuff there, but most of them wouldn't know something evil if it ran up and bit their eyeball. These same fools are always whining about how times now are so bad and how good they had it back when they were growing up. It was always better times. Innocent times. Back in the thirties or forties or whenever, they were all sinless little babes and it was always springtime—except when they were walking six miles through the snow to get to school. And even then, the snow sparkled and everybody was rosy-cheeked and jolly and winter was one big happy snowball fight. We have snowball fights in the alley, all right, but you have to watch out or you will get your teeth knocked out when some guy packs a slush ball around a rock and blind-sides you in the face with it. In the summertime, you play in the alley and build stick forts for plastic soldiers or throw rocks at the garbage cans.

Our alley isn't like some fancy neighborhood alley, because we don't live in a fancy neighborhood. Our alley divides a block that has a few wood-frame multi-family houses with tiny yards and a couple of stucco apartment buildings, just two over two, so they weren't real tall. The apartment buildings like ours have little yards, too, where the grass won't sprout on the hard-packed clay and nobody tries to grow it anyway.

You can't skate in the alley. The pavement is all busted and cracked and there are big potholes that always seem to have black, greasy water in the bottom. And rusty nails and jagged metal straps from crates that had been busted open long ago. There are nasty sharp-toothed lids from tin cans and ripped-up chicken wire and probably a million broken bottles. Everything is nasty and greasy and ugly-scabby-groaty. If you fall down in the alley, you are going to get a bad cut and catch lockjaw or something worse.

The alley is darker than every place else. That's because it is so narrow— just wide enough for the trash collector's truck—and the garages and sheds and back fences throw a lot of shadows, too. It is dim no matter what time of day it is. Unless it is noon, of course, when the sun is straight overhead. Even then, though, the alley is always somehow darker than the rest of the world, as if the sun has to fight its way through a screen to reach the ground. Sometimes, the alley takes on a whole otherness. It is like you and the alley are on slightly different planes in the universe. Like your eyes have lost all depth perception and you are standing in front of a flat mural of the world. Or like if you take a step and your foot finds the ground half an inch lower than where you thought it is. It is a dark place and you are drawn to it.

Mom doesn't want you to play in the alley. Walt doesn't give a damn whether you play in the alley or in the middle of Highway 59, but Mom tries to keep you out of there. She says it is dangerous. Once that's said, you couldn't be kept away from it with barbed wire and guard dogs.

You have some favorite places in the alley, especially the garage behind your apartment building. The alley is on a lower level than the apartments, so the garage is pretty much below grade—essentially underground. Nobody parks a car in there anymore because the alley is so narrow that cars like Walt's Buick can't make the turn. Because the garage is below grade level, there aren't any windows, just side-hung doors like on a barn, and the floor is only hard-packed dirt—no cement. You find a way to get into it, though, by pushing one of the doors away from the frame where the bottom hinge has rusted away and you can wriggle through the opening. Inside, it is black dark except for a little light coming from around the doors. You dare yourself to squeeze through the door into the darkness and stay there, blind. Eventually you have a vision of yourself lying dead on the greasy dirt with rats tiptoeing over your body sniffing for the tasty parts. A clammy smell rises from the dirt floor and it feels like there is a cobweb across your face even when there isn't.

Another hideout is up the hill where the alley dead ends before Bales Street, the way blocked by an abandoned delivery truck. The truck is small, not much bigger than a station wagon, and it sits in the weeds under a sycamore tree behind a big old house where nobody is ever home. The truck isn't on blocks or anything but somebody has taken the tires and wheels and just left the truck sitting on its brake drums to rust away. The whole thing has sunk down into the ground right up to the running boards. You stomp down the weeds around the driver's side door and yank on it until you can crawl inside.

What you find in there makes you think there has to be a story about the truck. A story perhaps of a job tragically interrupted. The truck is loaded as if ready to make a delivery. The whole back of it, from the front seats to the rear door, is full of old newspapers. Not just thrown in there, either, but piled neatly like you stack them for the paper drive at school. It is a solid pile of old newspapers from the floor to the bottom of the windows in the rear door. Level, too, so you can lie down stretched out flat across it. There aren't any windows on the sides, but you can lie on those newspapers and look out through the dirty glass in the rear door just fine. The truck spooks the other neighborhood kids so they have never broken out the windows and the top hasn't rusted through yet, so the old heap is watertight and the newspapers are as dry as a dead wasp nest. Mice are the only creatures that have been in that truck before you. You can see where they nest in all that dry yellow newspaper. You lie in the truck and tell yourself spooky stories.

The other end of the alley has an excavation in the pavement behind a sawhorse that leaves just enough room for the trash collectors to get through. It is marked by a smudge pot smoldering next to the hole. It's a greasy black pot that looks like a cannon ball, only bigger, about the size of a soccer ball. The road crew fills it with kerosene and leaves it burning all night to keep cars from driving into the hole. It puts out a plume of greasy black smoke so it works in daylight, too. The best thing about the smudge pot is the flame, even though you can't see it in the sunshine. You gather twigs and broken boards and burn them in it. You aren't allowed to carry matches, but you don't need them.

The alley isn't your happy place. It is where you go to be alone with dark thoughts. A place that allows—no, demands—lightless visions of violent death and black play with a fire oozing greasy smoke and spying on the world through the smudged windows of an abandoned truck.

~~§~~

Somehow, Mom gets you a bike from the Salvation Army store and teaches you to ride on the school playground. It isn't new and shiny but instead red and rusty and clunky, with fat tires and a welded frame of heavy steel. It has red, white, and blue streamers on the handle grips, though, and a spring-loaded bell that rings jauntily despite its rust.

The bike is total freedom. It takes you to neighborhoods with fancy houses and tidy green lawns, to horn-blaring streets lined with multi-colored storefronts, to elm-shaded boulevards and, one day, up a long and wide hill crowned by a tall, vine-covered wrought-iron fence that encircles the hilltop like a secret stadium. From the street below, it looks as if the fence surrounds nothing. No building stands behind it, no roads lead to any gates through it. The fence juts black against the sky, spiked pickets sticking out of the leafy

73

vines like spears stabbing the clouds. Acres of mown grass lie around it—a park without benches or trees or walking paths. The street is silent, the summer air still, as you push your bulky bike across the grass up the hill to the fence. The closer you get, the more threatening its pointed barbs appear. The fence is meant to keep people out of something, not to decorate some expansive, topiary-studded estate. The fence threatens bloody impalement to anyone foolhardy or desperate enough to try to scale it. Tangled vines twist through the iron bars and screen whatever hides on the other side. You try to pull them apart to peek through, but they are too thick. Finally, you find a spot where something has stripped the vegetation of its leaves, leaving only stiff stems twisted through the bars and a narrow niche for a cramped peek at the mystery.

Your breath catches. Behind the fence stretches a deep concrete bowl as wide as a football field. Utterly empty except for weeds growing through the cracks in the gray concrete, the desolate bowl resembles nothing so much as a catch basin for God's tears. The desolate expanse frightens you. What giant would build such a thing? For what use? Why is it abandoned? Would someone or some thing return to it? What if it catches you spying?

As you gaze at the vacant expanse, you imagine it to be some secret military installation, a sunken missile battery where nuclear death squats beneath the concrete poised to howl into the sky. You drill for nuclear attacks in school, learn to duck under your desk and cover your head, and you feel the same shiver in your spine as you imagine the concrete splitting open so a hissing, steaming rocket can rise to launch position.

You shove your bike through the grass back to the street, eyes down, afraid to look back. The vision of the horrible vacant space stays with you for years even after you learn it was simply an abandoned reservoir, part of the city's old water system.

When we move to the basement of the tavern in St. Joseph, I spend as much time outside as I can. There isn't any yard to speak of, just a junk-strewn vacant lot next door, but my bike gives me freedom to explore the rest of the world. That is how I find Corby Pond.

To get there, I ride north on Twenty-Second Street, down the hill through the first few blocks of tiny, neatly kept homes, then on a level stretch to the railroad tracks. The street begins a slow climb from there through what was known as "Goose Town", the African-American neighborhood in the town's dying center. You have to remember that St. Joseph is a backward town in a former slave state and attitudes die hard. It may have been a hundred years past, but people in town still boast with perverse pride that Abraham Lincoln wouldn't (or at least didn't) cross the river from Kansas to speak there when he ran for President. None of that matters to me. I am perfectly at home in the black neighborhood, a skinny crewcut white boy on a big red bike. I always stop when I reach the heart of the area at Messanie Street because the hills get steeper there and I can't climb them without a rest. I get a drink of water from the Sinclair station on the corner, nod my thanks to the one-eyed black man sitting in the shade of the building, then get back on my bike.

The big Sears store at Messanie Street marks the beginning of heavier traffic that continues past Bee Wayne's Bakery, home of the world's best cake donuts with chocolate frosting, and then the gas station with an enigmatic billboard advertising "Pink Air Coming April, 1966." That date comes and goes with no resolution to the existential question. The words just disappear in May of that year under a coat of white paint.

The pedaling gets harder as I continue the climb past the nice homes north of Jules Street. It levels off some at the Frederick Avenue intersection and traffic gets heavier, too. Hatfield's Hardware and Sporting Goods is on the west side of Twenty-Second Street. They sell guns and fishing tackle and a smattering of camping gear I desire but can't pay for. Hatfield's has a Western Auto franchise, too, so there are loads of tools and auto accessories to browse through. It is a place bound to please a boy.

Once I get past the traffic light at Frederick, I am on the homestretch to Corby. It is still an upgrade, but not as bad, and the street is shaded by big trees and lined with ever-nicer homes as I get closer to the wealthier section of town. If I pass the turn to Corby Pond and stay on Twenty-Second Street, it eventually ends at Lover's Lane, the street made famous by Eugene Field's treacly poem. That's where the doctors and other seriously rich folks live.

Corby Pond, though, is my destination. I turn onto the parkway and follow it to where a grassy bank runs from the street down to the water's edge. A rough foot path leads around to the opposite side of the pond. Trees and undergrowth lend an air of dark concealment contrasting with the open parkland on the street side of the water. Aside from the occasional used condom and a few rusty beer cans, the trail shows little sign of human use. I fish from that side of the pond sometimes, but it is hard to cast a line with all the tree limbs crowding the water, so I generally stay on the street side. The opposite corner of the pond is far enough away from the sparse traffic on the parkway to enjoy the solitude that is the real attraction of fishing for me.

I fish mostly with dough bait I make myself. The hard-packed vacant lot we call a yard never yields any night crawlers and I sure don't have money to buy them from the bait counter at Hatfield's, so I mix up a fist-sized wad of smashed corn flakes, flour, water, and vanilla extract for scent. Let it set for a few minutes until it gets gummy, put a glob on a treble hook and sink it to the bottom, and you can catch a catfish or a carp. Get hungry enough and you can nibble on it yourself.

The biggest challenge of fishing this way is casting the bait and line. My rod and reel are hand-me-downs, gifts from Jack, far from the latest technology. The rod is tapered steel, not something you'll find in the Orvis catalog. The bait casting reel has a spool, crank, drag, and level rewind mechanism. It is a true test of a fisherman's coordination. To use it successfully, you need an educated thumb and a confident arm. On the back swing, the drag is off so you keep the reel from unspooling with your thumb. Then you fling the rod tip toward your target and lift your thumb at the perfect time to let the line spool off. As the line speeds out, you feather the spool—again with your educated thumb—to match the speed of the free-wheeling reel to the decelerating flight of the baited hook and sinker. If you jam down your thumb too soon, your bait goes flying off the hook. Too late, and the line snarls as it stops flying out while the reel keeps spinning. The resulting bird's nest can take hours to unravel. Eventually, I get a Zebco spin casting reel with a fiberglass rod. It costs three dollars and almost never snarls, but casting with it doesn't give me quite the same sense of accomplishment.

I never catch much of anything. The dough bait sometimes attracts a small channel catfish, but it's seldom big enough to eat and I don't really want to ride back home with a dead fish dangling from the handle bars on my bike and slapping against my knees. I wiggle the treble hook until it pulls free and toss the fish back into the water. I don't care. I rebait my hook, cast back into the pond, and prop my rod up on a forked stick stuck into the ground. It's quiet and safe. I eat my peanut butter and jelly sandwich on white bread and contemplate nothing. Later, I'll retrace the route on my bike back to the tavern basement.

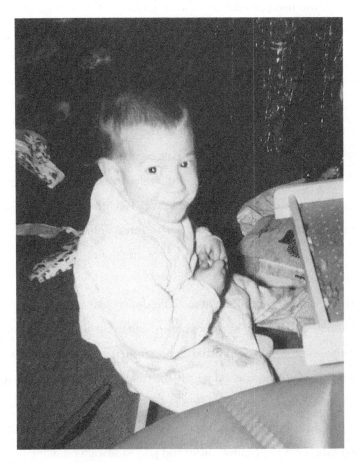

Ken, c 1962

Ken

Bible people in robes and sandals walk along a dusty road toward Bethlehem. Joseph leads a donkey carrying Mary up to a Roman soldier seated behind a rough table in the shade under a tree. Scenes of the Nativity fill the screen as a voice tells us that Judea has been ruled by Rome for a hundred years, but the prophets have said that a Redeemer would be born to bring them salvation.

I watch *Ben Hur* with a neighbor couple, friends of my mom, who sit with me between them in the dark theater on Independence Avenue. I am only eight years old, but even to me it is weird that these two grownups would take me to the movies, especially the night before Christmas. They are nice folks and everything, but I figure they really did it because Mom must want me out of the apartment for a while. Maybe she knows Walt is going to be in a bad mood. She always tells me to go to the store or go outside and play when he starts to get mean. Maybe that's why she sent me to the movies on Christmas Eve. I try not to think about anything but the movie.

The voice keeps telling about Jesus times and the Romans. I know the story of Jesus, of course; we talk about it all the time in Sunday school, but I don't know what he has to do with this Ben Hur guy. The posters in the theater lobby showed four white horses pulling a chariot in front of an ugly statue with a bunch of Roman soldiers and people in robes and stuff standing around. There wasn't a cross or anything else about Jesus in the movie poster.

Finally, the Nativity scene changes to a Roman riding through the streets leading a big army. The screen says *"Anno Domini XXVI."* I don't know what that means, but it doesn't matter; the Romans are cool. Loud horns blare fanfares and drums beat out a heavy march while the Roman soldiers carry their banners on tall poles with eagles on top. I think maybe the guy on the horse is Ben Hur, but then someone calls him Messala. I know from the way he talks about crushing the Jews and stuff that he is the bad guy.

The neighbors walk me home after the movie. Like us, they don't have a car. You can walk or get around pretty well in Kansas City on the bus if you have to. It is a cold night, but there isn't any snow. Mom made me wear my big coat, wool cap, mittens, and a scarf—all of it over a tee shirt, long-sleeved shirt, and a sweater! I leave my coat open on the way home and don't put the ear flaps down on my cap so I don't look like a total fruit. As we walk, the neighbors ask me what part of the movie I liked best and I tell them it was the chariot race. Not when Messala got run over, but when Ben Hur made his horses jump over a big wreck and he got thrown over the front of his chariot and didn't even get killed. The battle with the ships was pretty neat, too.

Mom opens the door and invites the friends in, which is really weird. It is almost midnight! The living room is dark but I can see my stepdad, Walt, silhouetted in the doorway to the kitchen. He leans against the door frame, but he is holding a coffee cup instead of a beer, so everything is probably all right.

"Shhh," Mom said. "Wayne's asleep." Then she plugs in the Christmas tree. The red and green and blue bulbs make just enough light for me to see four plastic chariots frozen in mid-race on the floor. An army of miniature

Roman soldiers march in a line behind them. Some of them carry those banners with eagles on top of the poles. Excited, I flop down to look at them from floor level.

"Wow!" I say. "Just like the movie!"

"Santa came while you were gone, hon," Mom says. "What do you think? Did he do OK?" I roll over and jump up to put my arms around her waist and bury my face in her stomach.

"Thanks, Mom. This is great!"

"Don't thank me, thank Santa."

"Oh yeah. Okay." I had figured out Santa last year, but it didn't hurt to play along because it made Mom feel good. I look up at her. "I can use these with my Alamo fort. Can I get it out now?"

"Oh no, you don't," she answers with a smile. "It's way past bed time and we've got a long bus ride to Franny's tomorrow. That's why Santa left your present early. Off to bed, now."

"Aw, Mom. Just for a little bit. Please?"

"That's it, buddy," Walt says. "Get yourself to bed."

I know better than to argue, so I head off to the bedroom I share with Wayne. The neighbor couple wishes me a merry Christmas and I hear them telling Mom I was a little angel during the movie. I close the bedroom door, put on my pajamas, and crawl into bed. Wayne breathes softly with a little snuffle from a cold. I try to stay awake thinking about how I could set up the tin Alamo walls so it would look like the chariot race place, but I drift off.

~~§~~

That spring Ken is born and the next year we get a car, a clunky old Buick without fins, but at least we can go places without the hassle of the bus. Walt drives us to Aunt Franny and Uncle Ray's house in Gallatin, a really

81

small town about an hour from Kansas City, and leaves us there for a couple of weeks after school lets out for the summer. Mom says he has to go back to Kansas City to keep looking for work. Mom says we all need some fresh air and Aunt Franny's house is the best place she knows to get it.

My Uncle Ray manages the co-op feed store in Gallatin. He is a big, tall guy with short curly hair and strong hard hands made rough by throwing around heavy sacks of feed. Aunt Franny is tall, too, but kind of skinny. She works in her garden and cleans her house all day long. Mom says Aunt Franny's house is cleaner than a hospital operating room and weeds won't grow in her garden because they are afraid of her.

I like my aunt and uncle. They look tough but they aren't that way at all. My cousin Terry and I wait on the porch for Uncle Ray to come home from work. When we hear his truck, we hide behind the bushes on either side of the steps and hold our breath until he comes up the sidewalk. Then we jump out and each of us grabs one of his legs and holds on tight. It is like hugging a walking telephone pole. Uncle Ray is so strong he just keeps on walking as if he didn't have a kid wrapped around each of his legs. He marches right up the steps and into the house and tells Aunt Franny he worked so hard today that his legs feel like they are stuck in cement. Then he looks down and pretends he just noticed us. That's the signal for each of us to grab one of his hands and get swung up onto his shoulders. He lifts us both at the same time and laughs while he does it.

Aunt Franny is real nice, too, although she's pretty strict about washing your hands and face and saying your prayers and stuff like that. Mom calls her "Sarge" because she'd been in the Women's Army Corps during the war. Mom says that when I was a baby we lived with Aunt Franny and Uncle Ray, but I don't remember that.

Aunt Franny really likes babies. You can tell by the way she stops whatever she is doing whenever Ken pulls himself upright and takes a couple of steps. He is just learning to walk. He crawls over to a chair or something else to hold on to, then stands up and lurches away from it. He usually takes about three steps before he loses his balance and sits down hard on his behind. He does it so often he isn't even surprised anymore and just sits there and laughs. Aunt Franny always cries "Boom!" when he plops down and that makes him laugh even more. After a couple of days, he starts saying "Boom!" himself whenever he sits down. Then he claps his hands and laughs so hard sometimes he rolls right over on his round bottom.

I am just a year younger than my cousin Terry, but he is about a head taller than me. We roam all over Gallatin on our bikes. I get up in the dark before the sun rises to help him with his paper route. One morning after we have delivered all the newspapers, Terry and I stop on the way home to try the new slingshots Uncle Ray had made for us. We sneak into one of the neighbor's gardens and fill our pockets with green grapes. They make great ammunition because they are just about the size of marbles and pretty hard. They are lots better than rocks. We walk our bikes along the gravel road, stopping every now and then to take a shot at a fence post or one of the glass insulators high up on a telephone pole.

There is a big corn field next to Aunt Franny's house and the utility wires that run along the road are always full of birds. When we get there, Terry points at the line of birds on the wire above us, loads his slingshot and fires almost straight up. He misses and the birds don't even flutter. I start to snort a laugh then clamp my hand over my mouth to keep from startling the birds.

"Come on, smarty," he whispers. "Let's see you do it."

I pull a handful of grapes out of my pocket and pick through them until I find one that's perfectly round and slightly larger than the rest. I stretch the band back to my nose and sight in on a fat black starling on the wire ahead. When I release it, the grape sails along a shallow arc directly at the bird. It seems to go into slow motion at the end of the flight just before it strikes. The starling's feathers muffle the sound and the grape falls to the ground. The bird doesn't move for a second, then it just slips off the wire and flutters to the ground as the rest of the flock explodes into the air and sweeps away over the corn in the whir of a thousand wings.

"Hey, cool!" Terry shouts as we bolt for the spot in the road where the bird flops weakly in the dust. "Great shot."

Terry and I squat on our heels and peer down at the starling. I can't see any blood or anything, but I know it is just about dead. Terry doesn't say a word. I reach to pick it up and he knocks my hand away. "Cooties" is all he says. The starling lays in the dust on its side. It jerks its head until one eye looks right at me. My breath catches and comes shallow when I see what I have done. The bird's eye is bright red and a single drop of blood squeezes out beneath it like a red teardrop.

Ken has been crying and fussing for several days. He doesn't want to eat and Mom has to rock and rock him to get him to settle down. Even then, he sleeps only a little while before he wakes up crying again. Finally, Uncle Ray drives Mom and the baby to see the only doctor in Gallatin. Mom says I can go but I have to be quiet.

The doctor is a rumpled old guy with gray hair and glasses. He wears a white shirt with the sleeves rolled up and a vest that is unbuttoned so his stomach can poke through. His office is full of sturdy and very old oak furniture. The examination table is a wooden platform padded by a folded wool blanket covered with white paper from a role at the end. The only decoration on the wall is a calendar from Uncle Ray's feed store. The doctor looks in the baby's eyes and ears and mouth. He takes his temperature and blood pressure and listens to his heart. Ken squirms and whimpers the whole time. The doctor asks Mom if the baby has diarrhea and tells her to give him plenty of fluids. He said there isn't any fever, so it probably isn't anything serious like a bad appendix, maybe just an upset stomach or a little gas. He says to come back in a couple of days if nothing changes.

We go back to Aunt Franny's, but Mom is still worried. Aunt Franny says that the doctor is a good man and has probably seen hundreds of babies acting just like this. Besides, he is the only doctor in town. If Mom wants to see someone else, she'd have to drive to St. Joseph or clear back to Kansas City. Mom tells Aunt Franny she doesn't want to do that because Walt is there.

The baby fusses all that night and the next day. He won't eat and when they try to get him to drink some water, he just keeps spitting it back out. Then he turns his head away and clamps his little lips shut. It is Wednesday, so after supper all of us except Mom and Ken go to prayer meeting. I feel guilty because I am glad just to get away from the crying for a while. But Aunt Franny says she is going to ask the pastor to say a special prayer for the baby and we should all use our silent prayer time to do the same. That makes me feel better. I decide to add some more prayers before I go to bed. Jesus is sure to hear them since there are so many people asking him for the same thing.

Mom looks worn out and sick herself when we get home. Aunt Franny mixes a little sugar in the baby's bottle and he finally takes a few swallows. Then she adds a little whiskey to the sugar water to settle his stomach and help him sleep. He manages a couple more swallows and slips off to sleep with the nipple still in his mouth. Mom finally falls asleep in the rocker with the baby on her lap. Aunt Franny leaves them both to sleep in the chair and we all go to bed.

"Dear Jesus," I pray from my bedside in Terry's room, "Please make Ken get better and don't let Mom be sad anymore. I love you, so please make the baby feel better. I know you can do it. Thank you. Amen." I climb under the covers and finally go to sleep.

Mom's shrieks rack the house and I jolt awake. I can't get my bearings at first, then I remember where I am and scramble out of bed and run to her room. Aunt Franny dashes through the door just ahead of me and falls to her knees in front of Mom's chair. She leans over the baby laid across Mom's lap.

"He's not breathing!" Mom cries. "Do something, Franny!" I step closer and see the baby's body weakly jerking. His face is turning from red to blue. Aunt Franny sticks a finger in his mouth and pulls it open. She covers his mouth and nose with her mouth. Then her cheeks puff out as she breathes into the baby's lungs. She lifts her head, takes a deep breath, and does it again. The baby whimpers faintly.

"Oh my God, Franny, what's wrong with him?" Mom pleads. She lifts the baby to her shoulder and rocks him gently.

"I don't know, but we better get him to a hospital," Aunt Franny says. "That was a convulsion!" She is still on her knees and reaches up to lay her hand softly on the baby's back. Ken gags and stiffens under her touch. Aunt Franny snatches him away and lays him on the floor as his spine snaps into an arch. Again she opens his mouth with her finger and blows air into his lungs. When his little body slumps back to the floor and he takes a breath on his own, she looks at Mom and asks if she can manage the drive to the hospital in St. Joseph while Franny works to keep Ken breathing.

Uncle Ray stays with us while Mom and Aunt Franny speed away in his truck. I am so shocked and frightened I am numb. All I see in my mind is the baby jerking up and down on the floor. Uncle Ray sits down in the rocker and pulls me onto his lap.

"That's OK—go ahead and cry," he murmurs into the top of my head pressed against his chest.

"I'm scared, Uncle Ray."

"I know you are. But don't worry. The Lord Jesus will take care of you and the baby and your Mom," he whispered. "Sweet Jesus takes care of us all."

We sit around the next morning, waiting to hear what happened. Uncle Ray says there isn't anything we can do but wait and pray. Terry turns on the TV but there isn't anything to watch. They only get one channel from Kansas City and it has some stupid show about cooking with a woman wearing a dress and an apron and a pearl necklace. She looks like she is getting ready to go to church. I never saw my Mom or any other lady I know dress like that when they were cooking dinner. Terry turns it off and puts on the radio. "I Fall to Pieces" is playing and then the station gives the news. It is all about the Russians building a wall in Berlin.

Terry turns it up louder when they start talking about sports. Stan Musial is my favorite player but Terry is a Cubs fan and he likes Ernie Banks, even though he is a Negro. Uncle Ray says they are both real heroes because they don't play for money, they play because they love the game. He says Stan Musial even asked for a salary cut last year because he didn't play very well the year before. Uncle Ray says that showed what a fine man he is. The radio says that both teams won yesterday. The Cubs beat the Dodgers and the Cardinals beat the Giants.

Aunt Franny finally calls right before lunchtime. She tells Uncle Ray that the baby just came out of the operating room and will be in intensive care until he starts breathing better on his own. Uncle Ray hands me the phone and Aunt Franny tells me Mom is okay but she can't talk to me right now because she is sleeping in the waiting room. I don't understand everything, but Uncle Ray explains it as best he could. The baby had gone into convulsions three more times on the way to the hospital. That's why Mom was driving; so Aunt Franny could give mouth-to-mouth and keep him alive. A doctor rushed the baby right into the operating room and, when they cut in, they found a blockage in his intestine that had become gangrenous and a really high fever had set in. That's what caused the convulsions. No one knows what caused the blockage. The doctor said it is just one of those things that happens sometimes.

After lunch we sit around and listen to the radio some more, waiting for word from the hospital. Then Terry remembers something.

"Hey Dad! Can we go to the movies? *Ben Hur*'s playing."

"Sure, that's a good idea," Uncle Ray says. "It don't do no good to just sit around here waiting for the phone to ring. That sound good to you?" He looks at me where I sit cross-legged on the floor.

"Yeah. Sure. OK," I answer. I have already seen the movie, of course, but there was some neat stuff in it like the sea battle and the chariot race. It is weird that the movie is just now getting to Gallatin, but I realize that everything is a little behind here. Terry even wears a coonskin cap sometimes, even though Davy Crockett was over on TV and the guys in Kansas City stopped wearing them more than a year ago. Uncle Ray gives us each a dollar and drops us off at the movie theater after dinner. He asks the lady at the ticket window how long the movie lasts and says he'll be back to pick us up when it is over. He tells me not to worry because Jesus is looking after the baby and he will be all right.

We get some popcorn and Pepsi and settle into our seats in the dark theater. I try to concentrate on the movie and stop thinking about Mom and the baby. I do pretty good for a few minutes, but when Baby Jesus cries in the manger, it reminds me of Ken. I close my eyes and try to pray for him. Like Uncle Ray said, I pray to the Lord Jesus to make the baby get well and come home soon. I pray, but I don't really feel much better. I am confused.

There are too many thoughts running around in my brain and I can't hold on to any of them.

At the end of the movie, the Romans nail Jesus to the cross and hoist it upright. The sky goes dark and big clouds roll in and Judah Ben Hur watches with a bewildered, frightened look while the music wells up and turns real sad. I start crying but turn my head away from Terry so he won't see. I cry for Jesus and hate the Romans. It is all so unfair.

Judah's mother and sister, Miriam and Tirzah, go with Esther into a cave to escape the storm. They cower in the cave as the sky turns black and the wind roars outside. A huge flash of lightening illuminates the cave and you see that the sores from their leprosy have been healed. They run their fingers over each other's face and start to cry. I cry, too, but silently. Miriam and Tirzah emerge from the cave and stand with their faces uplifted into the rain. The sweet waters wash over them as the storm abates and the sky lightens. The blood of Jesus trickles from the base of the cross to mix with a rivulet of water on the ground.

Three empty crosses stand atop the mound of Calvary, silhouetted against the brilliant sky. A shepherd drives his sheep past them at the base of the hill. A hard sob grips my throat and I can't hold it back so I rush out of the theater into the lobby. I slump against the wall by the door and the ticket lady comes over and kneels to put her arms around me.

"What's wrong, honey?" she asks.

"My baby brother," I gasp. "He might be dead!" The blunt fact strikes me full force and I sob. My eyes are blinded by my tears but I hear her and the popcorn guy and then Terry trying to make me feel better. Uncle Ray comes and takes us home.

~~§~~

Nothing smells as good as the feed store. It smells toasty and hearty and incredibly complex. The sweet decay of newly-mown grass, an acrid whiff of leaves burning in the fall, even the rich aroma of baking bread are all in the dust that fills the air. Cracked corn, oats, barley—even sunflower seeds—all get lightly toasted by the friction of grinding and mixing and bagging and the air sparkles with their dust. Each grain lends a separate scent to the mix and makes the air almost thick enough to chew. It's like breathing cornflakes.

Terry and I hang around the feed store a lot that summer. I stay with Aunt Franny and Uncle Ray while Mom goes back to Kansas City to take care of the baby. He is still real sick and needs a lot of rest and quiet. I miss Mom and the baby, but I understand why it is best for Wayne and me to stay in Gallatin. Besides, Walt is home with Mom sometimes and she says he isn't in a very good mood so it is probably best to stay where I am. Anyway, it is summer and there are lots of things to do in Gallatin.

Besides delivering Terry's papers and hanging around the feed store and going to church and Sunday school, we play *Ben Hur* a lot. Uncle Ray lets us make two swords from scrap wood we find behind the feed store. We cut shields out of a big corrugated carton and tie them to our arms with rope. There is a dense bush in Aunt Franny's front yard that we hack and stab over and over again like it is a gladiator. It is really neat because your sword goes right in when you jab the bush and then sticks there with the handle poking out like you have driven it through some Roman soldier's chest.

Aunt Franny catches us, though, and lays on a real tongue lashing. She yells something about her "favorite forsythia" and yellow flowers in the spring and how we have ruined it for next year. When Uncle Ray comes home, she tells him we need a good paddling because we beat up her bush. He takes us out behind the shed but, instead of whacking us on the behind like he usually did, he smacks his own thigh a couple of times to make a noise to fool Aunt Franny.

"Now, don't you tell on me, you two," he whispers with a little grin. "I hate that doggone bush. A forsythia ain't nothing more than the king weed of the bush family. But, as much as I'd like to see you beat it to pieces, you better lay off or Franny will give you a smack herself. Now, get on out of here."

One of the best *Ben Hur* things we do is chariot races on our bikes, riding real fast around the cinder track at the school grounds and pretending to run over the other charioteers and stuff. We swerve from one side of the track to the other like we are dodging around wrecked chariots and dead horses. Terry and I take turns being Ben Hur and Messala. Being Messala is cooler because you tie a stick to each of the saddlebag baskets on the rear wheels so they jut out like the knives on Messala's chariot wheels in the movie. You can run over people and chop them in half and maneuver your knives into their wheels and grind them up so they crash. It is cool. Eventually, I get lost in the fantasy and ride up beside Terry like Messala trying to wreck Ben Hur. I pedal alongside him and maneuver closer.

"Hey, watch it!" he yells when he sees what I am doing. He stands on his pedals for more speed but so do I. The cinders shoot out behind our tires.

"Look out, stupid!" Terry tries to swerve away but there is a curb and he can't. I give it an extra push and jerk my bike to the left. I try to rub the stick against his back tire, but instead it flips into the spokes. The stick snaps with a loud crack and Terry's tire locks and he flies over the handlebars. The basket rips off my bike and I fall over sideways onto Terry's. His handlebar jabs into my ribs real hard and my elbow grinds into the cinders on the track.

"Look what you did, you fart!" Terry screams. He had broken his dive with his hands and now they are skinned and bloody with cinders struck in his palms. His chin is all scraped up, too. He gets to his knees and inspects his hands, fighting back tears and trying to think of something else to call me. I crawl off his bike and onto the grass next to the track.

"I'm sorry," I say. "Are you hurt?"

"What do you think, stupid?" He shows me his bloody palms.

"Me, too." I hold out my hand to him and then lift my shirt to see if I am bleeding.

"You are such a butt hole," he says.

"I said I was sorry. Besides, you were Ben Hur and you weren't supposed to fall."

"Yeah, right. Like I could keep going with that stick in my wheel. Hey, look what you did to my bike!"

The handlebars on both bikes are twisted off center and the wire baskets are mashed. Terry's is worse, though, because two spokes are torn out of the back wheel and some others are bent and just barely hanging by one end. Terry yanks them out so the wheel can turn. We start the long walk home, pushing our bikes as best we can. Terry's t-shirt is spotted with blood from his chin and smeared with blood and black specks of cinder from where he wiped his hands on it.

Aunt Franny makes us both sit still while she washes our scrapes and picks the cinders out of our skin. That hurts. But what really hurts is when she paints iodine on our palms. That stings so bad we squeeze our eyes shut and cry "Ow-w-w-w" while we blow on them to stop the burning. When Uncle Ray comes home, he just shakes his head.

~~§~~

The summer ends and school is about to start when I finally go home. Mom crushes me to her chest at the front door and brushes her hand through my crew cut, pressing my face against her neck. My throat tightens up. She pushes me back to arm's length so she can see my face.

"Did you have a good time at Aunt Franny's? Were you good?"

"Yeah, it was okay. But I'm glad I'm home. Where's Ken?" I ask.

"He's in the crib. Let me look at you first. I missed you so much."

She sits on the couch and pulls me down next to her. She tells me that there were some things that I should know about. Ken's just fine, she says, but he's different now. When he had the convulsions, his air was cut off and his brain didn't get as much oxygen as it needed. So he lost something inside his head and he is different from the way he used to be. I don't really understand what she means. She takes my hand and leads me to the crib.

It is dark and quiet in there. We stand still while our eyes adjust to the dim light. I can hear the baby breathing soft and sort of raspy. Mom lifts a window shade just a little and I see him lying on his back under a blanket in the crib. He doesn't look any different to me and I touch the hand he is clenching to his chest. His hand doesn't move but his eyes open for a second. He looks at me but I can see he doesn't recognize me. His eyes are blank. Mom holds her finger across her lips and we go back into the living room.

"What's wrong with him?" I ask.

"They don't know for sure yet, but he's back to being like a brand new baby now. He doesn't see very well and he doesn't talk or walk or even crawl."

"Will he get better?"

"Sure he will, honey. We just have to pray for him a lot." She looks back into the room with the crib and her voice drops. "Right now, he's always peaceful. He doesn't even cry."

After his nap, I try to play with Ken, but he just lies there and looks at me without changing expressions. I stop asking Mom questions because I can see they are getting her down. I know she is trying to be cheerful so I won't feel bad, but her face sags every time I ask something else.

That night I toss in bed, sleepless with my unasked questions. Is he going to grow up? Will he ever start walking again? Will he say "Boom!" like he did at Aunt Franny's? The questions won't stop rolling through my head.

Mom had hung a cross Uncle Ray gave me on the wall above my head. It is plastic and, when the lights are out, it glows softly white with violet around the edges. The longer the lights stay off, the weaker it glows. Uncle Ray said it would help me remember the Baby Jesus every night as I go to sleep. The cross keeps drawing my gaze as I toss in bed. I try to thank Jesus and I try to pray like I had so many times that summer, but it just won't come out right. I am mad, like Ben Hur. I want to lash out at someone about Ken, but I don't know who. Uncle Ray had said it wasn't anybody's fault and Aunt Franny told me it was just one of those things that happened.

But they are wrong. My baby brother isn't something that just happened. This isn't a ball game where I can just shrug my shoulders and say, "Oh, well. Maybe next time." He isn't going to have a next time. Jesus isn't going to make him better. That was just a movie.

Brothers, c 1966

c 1959

Growing Up

Jeremy with his Great-grandmother Donelson,
1974

Religion

We never practiced much religion. Like most people, we professed belief in God but didn't invest any time or effort in it. I don't recall ever going to church with Mom or Walt in Kansas City and we didn't say grace at the table or prayers at bedtime. At one point not long after Mom married Lou and we moved into the house on Jackson Street in St. Joseph, my twelve-year-old self decided we needed a little actual religion in our lives so Mom and Wayne and I went to a Presbyterian church within walking distance a few Sundays. It didn't take, though. I studied the church literature but it was more about who was in charge of what in the church bureaucracy than what God had to say about anything.

When I was really little, Jack would take me to Baptist services when I stayed with him every other weekend. It always seemed more like something we were supposed to do rather than something we wanted to do, though. There wasn't any pleasure in it. I enjoyed the music, though, and the church had a near-life-size replica of Michelangelo's *Pieta*. The utter sadness of the piece haunts me even today. What kind of loving God kills people? Is that any way to prove a point about love? And how can a grieving mother have any hope when he does? I know that faithful true believers can go through mental gymnastics to prove the murder of Jesus is our ticket to heavenly bliss, but I'm not buying it.

The closest I ever came to a religious breakthrough was when my brother Ken suffered the illness that damaged his brain. The movie *Ben Hur* had just been released and it dominated my imagination for months. The doomed galley slaves propelling the ships into battle, the spectacular chariot race, the horror of the leper colony, the swelling of the music as Christ died on the cross silhouetted against the turgid sky—these images still twist my heart.

We also happened to be staying with my Aunt Franny and her devoutly Lutheran husband, my Uncle Ray, who not only mouthed the creed but believed it. Ken's screams of pain and the panicked response of the adults hovering over him became all mixed up in my mind with prayers and pleas to God that went unanswered. Unless, that it, there is a higher purpose in snuffing out the future mental capacity of a perfectly normal, happy two-year-old. He survived the oxygen deprivation that ruined his brain, but just barely. Ken couldn't walk until he was four and he never learned to read. How did God profit from that little trick?

Maybe He was trying to teach us something. To show us we can endure the anguish of hearing a baby's tortured screams if we just focus on God's greatness. Or that we can tolerate even the disabled among us to matter how needy and consuming they may be. Or maybe He was just proving to us that He can do whatever the hell He wants to whomever He chooses because He is omnipotent. Then there is the possibility He was testing the strength of our love for Him by seeing if we would worship Him despite the heartbreak He so casually inflicts. Regardless of the purpose, twisting a baby's intestines into a gangrenous knot was a sick page in God's glorious plan.

Eventually I pushed my feelings about God's role in Ken's fate to the back of my mind and tried to look at religious belief objectively. I read about the world's great and not-so-top-of-the-charts religions trying to find one that resonated with me. I found instead that Taoism, Protestantism, Animism, Judaism, all the isms, have the same overarching purpose: to empower their leaders to dictate how its followers are to live. The rules may well be edifying; love thy neighbor, do unto others, etc., etc., but they all represent nothing more than the imposition of rules on people that they probably follow anyway for the good of the tribe. The codification of the rules, though, and the investiture of authority over them gives the church leaders tremendous power.

My conclusion that God can't exist except as an excuse for one man to dominate his neighbor is confirmed by history and the millions and millions of people killed in the name of one God or another. At first, I tried to tell myself that God wasn't the problem—it was organized religion that lead men to mass murder. The greater power, mystical and majestic but divorced from man's varied dogma, wasn't the cause of man's depredations. God is above them, beyond concern, simply a greater power than we could ever understand. Eventually, though, I realized that I was grasping at mythology, looking for some outside force to guide my own behavior or serve as a convenient excuse for it. There is not only no evidence such a force exists, but I couldn't conjure any non-rational faith within myself, either.

It was then I recognized my anger at God as the agent of Ken's sickness was just another way of acknowledging His existence and primacy. God could not have caused Ken's intestines to telescope if God doesn't exist. I let that conclusion sink in. There is no one to blame. No mortal perpetrator and no deity flicking a magic finger. And if there exists no one to blame, there can be no anger. What is, is. Accept it and cope with it.

I also realized that I have a lifetime of proof that I am solely responsible for my own actions. What happens beyond me, whatever outside forces and laws shape my existence, are simply part of the chaos of the universe, not the fine print of some greater being's master plan. When I came to this conclusion I was liberated. I no longer had to look over my shoulder to see if God and His self-appointed minions were watching. I can be as good (or bad) a man as I want and am capable of being. The responsibility is mine and so are the consequences.

Which brings me to the afterlife. The whole idea of heaven and hell is quaint. I suppose it serves as a comfort or a motivator to some people, but not for me. I can easily understand the desire to use it to explain what happens when we die because the scariest things we face are the ones we can't see. The great unknown is horrifying and lack of certainty is debilitating. Belief provides an anchor, however tenuous, to a definite outcome to life. I just can't sell myself on such an unfounded, unprovable, and highly unlikely proposition for the sake of faith, which contradicts certainty almost by definition. Even during my various encounters with my own mortality, I have never felt any need for insights into what comes next. Whatever it is, I'm ready for it. If I believe anything, I believe there is nothing next, and I'm ready for that, too. What has happened can't be changed and, in the case of death and its subsequence, what will be, will be. It serves no purpose to worry about it. The absence of concern is liberating.

It also helps me focus on the present. I like to think I've done some good in my time on earth and get an extra dose of satisfaction knowing that I did it because I'm a good person, not because some dictator with a Bible told me I could rack up more heavenly airline miles toward some angelic forever in the clouds by helping little old ladies cross the street. Good behavior, living a life that benefits others, is its own reward.

Brothers, c 1975

With Dick Crumpton at Pebble Beach

Best Friends

Dick Crumpton was my best friend, but I don't remember the day I met him. It must have happened in Mrs. Wray's sixth grade class at Ward School, probably because his last name and mine—Crumpton and Donelson—were close together alphabetically so we sat in the same row. Mrs. Wray, knowing that I was new to town and perceptive little bird of a teacher that she was, put us together for group assignments, too, taking advantage of Dick's good nature to introduce me to the new kids in class and the ins and outs of sixth grade society. The friendship she encouraged lasted until Dick's sad and early death.

Dick and I found numerous commonalities from the very beginning. We both read like fiends, played chess, were less than enthused about sports, and didn't have a lot of other friends. We became brothers by the end of the school year. We guarded each other's backs as comrades in arms against the world of playground bullies and the great mass of unwashed illiterates that offended our intellectual sensibilities. Yes, we were brain-power snobs of the first order.

Both of Dick's parents worked, his father for the telephone company, his mother as a teacher, so I thought they were rich. They must have been.

105

They lived in their own house—not an apartment—and had two cars. Dick even got an allowance. He was generous with it, too. When Van Gogh's "Night Sky" came to the Nelson Gallery in Kansas City, I stayed home "sick" the day of the class trip because Mom didn't have three extra dollars for the bus fare. Dick bought me a catalog of the show, though, and got everybody in the class to sign it.

His mom invited me to stay over for dinner on a regular basis even though I couldn't ask my Mom to reciprocate. A major treat in the Crumpton household was "shrimp night," when his dad would come home with a five-pound bag of shrimp that he had bought on sale. He boiled and served it heaped on newspapers spread in front of us on TV trays. We peeled and ate until we were stuffed, Dick and I washing ours down with Pepsi while his dad did the same with Pabst Blue Ribbon. In my limited experience, only rich people ate shrimp.

Dick and I did just about everything together. After school, we hung out at his house, watched TV, shot pool in his basement garage, and played a lot of chess on his set modeled after Medieval figures. Dick's mom, Lucille, was a short, rotund school teacher who scurried around the house in a state of perpetual lateness. She tried to compensate by setting all the clocks in the house ten minutes fast, which just exacerbated the problem. Dick inherited her off-kilter sense of time.

Whereas other guys played cowboys and Indians, Dick and I were inspired by Sir Walter Scott's *Ivanhoe* to take up jousting. We cut shields from cardboard boxes and fashioned swords out of sticks to stage mock battles in Bartlett Park. When I told Jack about it, he made us some "real" shields out of fiberboard filched from the sign shop at the Goetz Brewery where Grandpa Donelson worked. I painstakingly painted a big Maltese cross on mine. We were generally careful to aim our blows toward the other guy's sword and shield, but I carried a scar on my thumb for several years from one of Dick's wild swings. We also tried jousting on bicycles, but it was too hard to guide your bike while holding up a shield with one hand and aiming a broomstick lance with the other. It was just as well we couldn't do it; if we'd kept trying, one of us was sure to get a broomstick in the eye.

We even had girl friends who were best friends themselves. Patti, who lived up the street from Dick, was the love of my seventh grade life. On special occasions, Patti sported a pink poodle skirt and white cardigan while her friend, Theresa, wore a tight black leather skirt and fluffy angora sweater. They flirted with us in class and Dick and I dutifully responded by carrying their books home from Bliss Junior High, an idea I got from reading *Archie* comics in the barbershop next door to my grandmother's tavern. Neither romance lasted past seventh grade.

The summer Mom married Lou and we moved to the house on Jackson Street, Dick and I rode our bikes all over town. We usually met in Bartlett Park midway between our homes, pedaled to Krug Park in the north end of town—uphill all the way, it seemed—then came back through Bartlett along the parkway to Hyde Park in the south end of town, and finally returned to our starting point. It was a full day's ride on our three-speed Schwinns. Grandma got me the new bike for my birthday that summer to replace the clunky steel behemoth I had been riding.

Most times, we didn't do the full 37-mile round trip, preferring instead to linger in Krug Park where there was a lot to explore. A once-picturesque pond decorated the entrance to the park next to a parking circle where people fed the resident ducks. On the opposite side of the pond was an abandoned formal garden with arbors and paths between once-sculptured boxwoods now grown shapeless. Above the pond and garden was an Italianate field house on the verge of collapse. The fountains in the garden behind it were long dry, the esplanade cracked and leaf-blown, the pergola vine-less and rotting as it stood. The field house was once home to a circus-themed children's playground, but it was long abandoned. Like the rest of St. Joseph, Krug Park had seen its glory days come and pass it by, stopping only briefly for a moment in the spotlight. The Gilded Age companies in town had prospered and been passed down to the third generation of family owners, most of whom were well-satisfied with clipping bond coupons and living in sunnier and/or more sophisticated cities. They had no interest in continuing to build (or maintain) the town their enterprising forbearers had created, so treasures like Krug Park were in sad disrepair. Dick and I didn't care about its history, though, only that the decrepit field house in the park exuded the melodramatic air of an abandoned castle. Our imaginations reveled in possible story arcs.

It was a real test of manhood to pedal our bikes to the top of Krug Hill without getting off to walk them up the steep grade. We'd switch-back up the street, but when a car came along, we'd lose momentum and have to stop. Dick seldom made it all the way without pausing to rest, but I usually could, so I would sit at the top of the hill and wait for him. Looking down I could see the natural amphitheater and the stage, the old formal garden and the pond behind it, and the quiet city streets in the distance below. The natural amphitheater, completed in 1926 and one of the largest in the nation even today, could hold 25,000 people on its grassy slopes and park benches. I performed there in high school as part of concerts by the St. Joseph Symphony orchestra, playing my guitar and singing a few folk songs. The concerts were usually on warm Sunday evenings and they were free and therefore well-attended. The applause was adequate if not overwhelming.

Once Dick caught up with me at the top, the next test was to ride down the hill on the other edge of the park, swooshing around the treacherous curves and through the dark underpasses without touching our brakes—even once—until we got to the parking lot by the old field house. It didn't matter who made it to the bottom first, only that you did it right—no brakes! Our stomachs burned with adrenaline as we emerged from a dark overpass and leaned into the final steep curve high above the pond. One wobble and you could die. Use your brakes and you're chicken. We both always made it.

Foreshadowing our partnership on the high school debate team, Dick and I starred in a seventh grade play about the American Revolution that made the local newspaper. Dick played a dastardly British soldier while I portrayed a daring American spy. The newspaper sent a photographer who set up a scene where Dick searched diligently under a table for the spy (me) while I sat disguised as a woman next to it.

Junior high was a time of many firsts for us, but the one that stands out most vividly is when I had my first drink of liquor. It was New Year's Eve 1964 and Dick's parents were entertaining another couple from their neighborhood. The four of them played cards in the living room, smoking, drinking, and laughing around the folding table while Guy Lombardo and the Royal Canadians played on the TV in the corner. Dick and I hung out in his room playing Clue with Debbie, the daughter of the other couple, whom we knew from school. As the grownups partied and their celebration grew louder, our board game grew less and less interesting. Finally, Dick suggested we liven up our own little party. He told Debbie we were going to get some Pepsis and told me to come to the kitchen to help carry them back. When we got there, he told me to stand in the doorway so his mom couldn't see what he was doing. I leaned as casually as I could against the door frame and watched him pour Canadian Club into a water glass. When he got halfway to the top, he asked me if that was enough. I didn't have any idea, but I said "yes" with conviction anyway. He then topped it off with Pepsi, dropped in a couple of ice cubes, and did the same to the other glass. Then he filled one without whiskey for Debbie and we slipped back into his room.

It tasted real good. We kept looking at each other and snickering as the sweet whiskey went down and its warmth spread in our stomachs. Debbie didn't say anything but I could see she was curious about what was going on. I bent over to pick up the Clue game from the floor. When I stood up, my head reeled so I sat down right away to keep from falling over. Debbie smiled at me and I fell in love. I moved over and put my arm around her shoulders. She giggled a bit but didn't move away so I cuddled closer. Whiskey is great stuff, I thought. I grinned at Dick across the small room. He gave me a lopsided smile in return, then puked brown whiskey down the front of his yellow cardigan.

In high school, our group of friends expanded. Dick gravitated to the center of the circle while I orbited around it. I was drawn to the new world of folk music and low-grade hippiedom but Dick preferred the frat groups with guys from better-off families where I felt I didn't belong. It wasn't all in my imagination, either. Some of Dick's new friends were scions of local doctors, accountants, and business owners. Their mothers gave them allowances and bought them stylish clothes. Their fathers gave them cars. They were bound for college and wanted for nothing. Worst of all, they came between Dick and me. This fed my reverse snobbery and my need for recognition; my imperative to prove that I was better than my station. My relationship with Dick had validated my worth. Losing him to them undermined it. I plunged into theater and competitive speaking and the school newspaper and other activities where I could shine and re-validate myself. Dick and I stuck together for the debate team and I partied with him and his frat friends, but I also worked after school and weekends and I dated a few girls, so we inevitably spent time apart.

We went our separate ways for college but stayed in touch throughout. I married and Dick did too, eventually, and we re-established our deep friendship as we matured. I moved to New York but Dick and I spoke by phone almost daily for thirty-five years until his death in 2009. At least once a year for twenty years, we met someplace spectacular to play golf with our buddy Jim Lyons. We visited Palm Springs, Bandon Dunes, Pinehurst, Kiawah Island and numerous other fabulous destinations including Scotland, where we went to celebrate our fiftieth birthdays.

Dick was a good guy who came to a bad end. We grew up together, dealing with our individual demons during the hormone-ravaged years of puberty. We both suffered familial turmoil that the other one sensed but, in keeping with the tight-lipped stoic ethos of the time, we didn't talk about it. As children, we saw the bruises on each other's psyche without seeing the blows that caused them and applied the only balm we knew. We stuck together.

Lou, c 1966

Lou Again

We move into the house on Jackson Street when Mom marries Lou. It seems like we should be happy, indeed celebratory, and we are for a time. It is the first single-family house we have ever lived in, the achievement of the American dream, a step up into what to us is the solid middle class. And what a big step it is. My experience is of apartments. The first one with Walt over the grocery store, the second the four-room fourplex in front of the nasty alley before Mom left him, the most recent the dank cellar under the tavern from which we have now crept like prisoners from a dungeon blinking in wonder at the sunshine.

Lou, who freed us, seems a godsent savior. He has an infectious grin and big muscles. He is a fire fighter, an automatic hero to young boys and maidens alike. He drives a bright red 1956 Corvette that we can all miraculously fit into when Mom holds Ken, Wayne squeezes between her knees on the edge of the bucket seat, and I scrunch up and balance my bony butt on the console between Mom and Lou. All I have to do is keep my feet away from the gear shift knob where Lou rests his hand. Maybe someday he'll let me drive it, I think, while wriggling my arms even tighter around my knees to pull them to my chest and out of his way.

The splendid house is a wood-frame cracker box set on a concrete slab stretching the width of two cars parked on the street in front. But it has a yard with grass instead of cinders and a real bathroom with a real shower instead of a galvanized wash tub filled with water heated on the kitchen stove. There are two bedrooms and a closet-sized "sewing room" that will one day become my very own room. The living room has space for a spinet piano Mom hopes to have. There is no dining room, but the kitchen is large enough to eat in. The floors throughout are linoleum tile on the hard concrete slab, but they eventually get carpeted. Mom paints the walls and trim and makes curtains for the aluminum-frame windows. A stoop in front and a laundry room on the back and that is it—our own house.

Lou trades his Corvette for a '57 Chevy. It's a two-door hardtop and still pretty cool, but the two bench seats scream "family car" and Lou doesn't drive it with the same James Dean aura as he did the 'Vette. He promises to teach Mom to drive a stick shift so she can drive the '57, a shrewd move so he can later justify another Corvette as the family's second car. We don't care. To us, we are living a bourgeoise dream.

We live in the cookie cutter suburbs of St. Joseph where identical little houses are lined up one after the other on identical little plots for identical blocks and blocks. Our house has a lawn to mow, a tree with leaves to rake, and Lou cooks hamburgers and hot dogs on a charcoal grill in the backyard. I roam the neighborhood and play with kids that look just like me, shooting baskets in their driveways and catching crawdads in the creek that runs through the yards to the golf course on the other side of the highway a few blocks away.

~~§~~

Skateboards are just becoming popular and a few of the kids have them. I don't have money for a fancy one with hard rubber wheels and a molded platform, so I take apart my old metal roller skates and bolt the wheels to a piece of scrap lumber, creating a literal "skate board." It makes a lot of noise on the concrete street but I can go like hell down the long hill on the next street over. My primitive skateboard can't be steered since it doesn't pivot on the wheels like a store-bought one, but when I oil up the bearings, I fly.

Wayne is too little for a skateboard, but Mom gets him a bike. I watch as she guides him around in circles in the yard next door, which is level. At first he is scared and cries a bit but she reassures him and steadies him until he settles down and pedals while she runs behind holding him up. Soon he is giggling. It's the same way she taught me to ride a bike in Kansas City.

Lou comes out of the house and stands watching Mom trot along holding Wayne upright. "He ain't never going to learn that way," Lou says. Mom doesn't answer. Maybe she doesn't hear him. When they circle around under the neighbor's maple tree, Lou steps in front of them and grabs the handlebars. "I'll teach him," he says. Mom, confused and speechless, steps back and lets go of the bike seat. The bike starts to tip, so Wayne grabs the nearby tree trunk.

"Get off a minute," Lou says. Wayne shakes his head and tightens his grip on the tree. He doesn't know what to do. He can't get off the bike while he's holding on to the tree and if he lets go of the tree, he and the bike will fall over. He's scared of Lou, too. "Goddammit, get off!" Lou orders. Wayne shakes his head again and Lou grabs his wrists and forcefully peels his arms away from the tree. The bike falls between Wayne's legs as Lou lifts him clear. "Bring the bike, David." I jump to pull it upright and push it behind Lou as he drags Wayne to the top of the grassy bank that is our back yard.

"Lou, what are you doing?" Mom asks.

"I'm going to teach him how to ride this goddamn bike," he answers.

Our back yard slopes away from the house down to a gravel alley. I hate mowing that part of the yard because the only way I can do it is to push the mower parallel to the slope; it's too steep to shove the mower straight up and down the grade. It's not a big hill, maybe ten paces from top to bottom, but it falls steeply enough that we can lay down at the top and roll down it like logs, a game Wayne and Ken love. It's not fun now, though, as Lou sets Wayne on the bike facing down the slope.

I see that Lou is going to teach Wayne to ride a bike the same way Walt taught me to swim at the Salvation Army camp the day they came to pick me up. He asked me if I learned to swim that week, and when I said "no," he carried me over to the deep end of the pool and threw me in, clothes and all. "Paddle like a dog," he shouted while he clamped an arm around Mom's waist to keep her from jumping in to save me. Somehow, I didn't drown.

"Lou, please," Mom pleads.

He ignores her and gives the bike a quick shove to get it started down the hill.

"Pedal!" he yells as Wayne careens down the slope. Panicked, Wayne instinctively tries to stop by dragging his feet but they tangle with the pedals and he tips over half way down the bank. Mom runs to Wayne to see if he's hurt but Lou gets there first.

"Get up and stop your crying," he orders. He picks up the bike with one hand and pulls Wayne out of Mom's grasp with the other. Wayne isn't hurt. He sobs once, mostly from fear, then stops. Lou drags both him and the bike back to the top of the hill.

"No, Lou. Stop!" Mom cries. She steps in front of the bike.

"You treat them all like babies," Lou snaps. "He ain't hurt. Now get out of the way." He straddles the bike's rear wheel and manhandles Wayne onto the seat as Mom backs away. "Keep your damn feet on the pedals and steer straight," he orders. Before Mom can stop him, he pushes Wayne down the slope again. And once again, Wayne's feet fly loose and he tumbles off. He lays tangled in the bike, crying at the bottom of the hill.

"You gotta pedal, you son of a bitch!" Lou yells.

Mom wails. Lou tells her to get in the house. "He's just falling on grass," he says. "The little baby ain't gonna get hurt." She steps toward him in protest but he glares at her until she turns and brushes past me through the back door and into the house. I freeze, not sure what to do. I ought to stand up for my brother. Mom would be proud of me for doing that. But how can I? If Lou won't listen to her, he sure won't listen to me telling him to stop. And one back-handed swipe from his meaty hand would crush my face. I am scared. I am also stabbed by guilt when Wayne whimpers as Lou sets him on the bike and shoves him down the hill again. He does it again and again until eventually and inevitably, the bike one time stays upright and Wayne doesn't fall before he reaches the bottom. Lou turns his back without comment and goes into the house. I help Wayne push the bike back to the house and we store it next to mine under the eaves.

Lou builds a garage behind the house. Or rather, his father Roscoe builds it with Lou, Lou's son RL, and me as laborers toting boxes of nails and holding 2 x 4s steady while Roscoe frames the building. The garage has room for one car, Lou's vast tool collection stored in metal cabinets, a workbench, and an air compressor so Lou can paint cars. He keeps a cooler there, too, and some days he drinks an entire case of beer. Lou works at the firehouse every third day on a 24-hour shift and in a gas station the other two days. He spends nearly every other waking minute in the garage doing bodywork on someone else's car or puttering with his own.

I hang around, drawn by the manly mysteries of the place and hoping to maybe even learn about cars, but mostly trying to please Mom, who wants me to have some sort of relationship with Lou. I am generally in the way, though, and Lou admonishes me to not touch anything, especially the cars. "You won't see it, but your fingerprints on bare metal will show up when the paint goes on," he warns. I keep my hands in my jeans and find a place near the door to lean against the wall well away from the cars.

That's where I am the day the kitten comes to the garage. It is a hot, sun-glaring summer day and Lou has the overhead door open and the window fan running in the other end of the garage to create a breeze while he takes the tape off the trim around a fender he had painted the night before. The sun is brutal overhead and the kitten is looking for some shade. I see it from the corner of my eye and surreptitiously try to shoo it away with my hand. It is a fluffy yellow kitten with a white face and trusting eyes, obviously not old enough to know when it is in danger. It ignores the hand I flap at it behind my back. It takes a tentative step off the hot asphalt onto the concrete floor of the garage.

Lou pays no attention to me and doesn't see the kitten. He's intent on lifting masking tape off the car door trim with the tip of a knife blade without touching the paint. The fan roars steadily in the window and the radio blares steel guitar laments from KUSN. I take a chance and stamp my foot toward the kitten. Lou doesn't hear me, but neither does the kitten.

Sweat glistens on Lou's bare back above his jeans. It is just after lunch and he has been drinking beer steadily since mid-morning. Under his breath, Lou says, "Shit." Louder, he repeats it: "Shit. Shit. SHIT!" I freeze. So does the kitten. Lou drops the ball of tape and newspaper he has been wadding and leans closer to better see the surface of the fender.

"Shit," he says again. "Look at that, David." I panic. What did I do? How? When? "That's what happens when you touch the bare metal and don't wipe it clean. Shit!" I am reprieved. He must know it wasn't me. "Pay attention," he says. "I'm trying to teach you something."

I take a tentative step closer and bend forward to see the paint. I can't see the flaw he's fuming about but decide I'd better fake it. "Gosh," I say. "Now what?"

"I have to paint the fucking thing again," he growls. "You might as well start sanding." That's not good news. I will now spend the rest of the weltering afternoon painstakingly hand-sanding the paint off the entire door with 400 grit wet-or-dry sandpaper. That's the only thing he will let me do—in fact, makes me do—in the garage.

Lou gets another can of beer out of his cooler. He pops the top and takes a long, loud swallow. He belches softly and picks up the wad of paper and tape he had dropped. He takes another slug of beer and walks toward the door to put the trash into the barrel outside. The kitten mews as he gets to the doorway.

"What the hell?" Lou exclaims. "Get out of here!" He stomps his foot but the kitten doesn't move. Like me, it is paralyzed.

"You little shit," Lou mutters. He takes a single step and tries to kick the kitten in the ribs. He misses, mostly, but catches it a glancing blow that sends it tumbling across the driveway to the neighbor's yard. It crouches, frozen in fear, but finally limps away into the weeds. "Fuck you," Lou says, mostly to himself.

I keep my mouth shut and resist the urge to protest. What can I do? I can't say anything to him. Mom has married this man who bought us an American-dream house. He puts food on the table for three kids not his own—one of them disabled. Helpless and ashamed of it, I keep pushing the sandpaper.

(left to right) Bill Russell, Cecile, Frances (unknown)
(front) Barbara, Margie

River

The May sun twinkles a'play

On the rolling, roiling river,

It is a bluff cloud frontier,

The line between whiskey and beer.

Wild grape, cottonwood, and blackthorn locust,

Willow, sumac, poplar, and white trunk sycamore

Crowd along the rip rap levees

Like sentinels of the flat bottom land behind.

And then

The Blacksnake Hills with their yellow loess cliffs

Peer over the woods along the unstoppable river.

c 1960

Swing Bridge

Mom takes me down to the railroad bridge across the Missouri River to visit Dusty Roades, the man who operates it. He is a jolly, gentle, soul and Mom wants me to see another kind of man before I grow up and become one. She went to high school with Dusty and he's her best friend's husband and father of two daughters—one my age. Lou made him a pal because he moonlights as a track announcer at local speedways and he can get Lou in for free. I have gone to the track with them a couple of times. It's loud and stinks of burning rubber and hot oil. I don't really like it but I go and pretend I do because I am expected to.

Mom and I walk carefully along the tracks suspended over the river to a machine shed perched on a concrete pylon in the middle of the span. Like so many other things in St. Joseph, the bridge seems barely functional, a relic of days past when the town was an important place in the nation's westward migration. It was built about sixty years before we step foot on it. The span replaced the original bridge built in 1873. We pick our way through shadow lines cast by a lattice of iron trusses framing the span. I touch one of the thumb-size rivets holding them together and my fingers come away smudged with brown rust. The bridge sits maybe thirty feet above the river, not high enough for tugboats to pass under but high enough to kill you if you fall.

Dusty greets us when we open the door to the rickety machine shed. "Want to take a ride?" he asks. I look around but don't see anything except a control panel with some wheels and levers, a transistor radio, and windows overlooking the railroad track stretching from Missouri to Kansas over the river. I am thirteen years old and confused. I have never seen the bridge in operation.

Mom smiles some encouragement. "Go ahead," she says. "It's fun."

I still don't know what they're talking about and it must show on my face. "Come on," Dusty says. "I'll show you."

He opens the shed door and we walk on the ties toward Kansas. We stop where another concrete pylon supports the track midway between his shed and the river bank.

"Just sit right here," he says, pointing down to a small wooden platform on the ties between the rails. "You'll feel a little bump, then the bridge will move. Don't worry. It moves slow." I sit cross-legged on the platform. He starts walking back and tosses a warning over his shoulder. "Just don't stand up until it stops moving."

I nod. I look down between the ties at the blue-brown water rolling below me, white-capped in spots, carrying small rafts of tree branches and other debris downstream. It's hot in the sun but the river doesn't look cool. A breeze from Kansas carries the smell of field dust and hot diesel. The ties give off a thick odor of creosote and the steel rails are hot to the touch. The bridge jolts into motion and a space opens in front of me between the ends of the track where I'm sitting and the rest of the track reaching into Kansas. With a rumble of gears I feel in my spine, the track swings slowly sideways until I am facing upriver, nothing before me but the muddy water.

I see now how this section of the bridge pivots to let boats and barges pass. It's an engineering marvel and I sit cross-legged on the end of it, a speck on the timeline of industrial achievement. When the track stops moving, I stand, turn, and look back at Mom and Dusty in the machine shed. I grin and wave to let them know I am all right.

But I am not all right. When I turn back to face the river, I make the mistake of looking over the end of the track at the water flowing below. The thick river moves in mesmerizing swirls. The current flows one way but the wind ripples against it the other way and unseen snags and sand bars beneath the surface push it into spinning eddies. My eyes swim with the erratic motion. I try to focus them by staring harder, but the bits of debris in the water seem to run faster and the swirling behind my eyes speeds up, too. I try closing my eyes but that only makes it worse so I open them quickly. Unsteady, I sway on my feet in the hot wind. I need a railing to hold on to, but there is nothing to grasp. Trying not to panic, I force myself to stare at the steady horizon beyond the levee. Slowly I kneel, careful to look anywhere but down at the roiling water. When I sit back down, the track lurches and begins its slow arc back to close the span. When it stops with a jolt, I breathe again.

I step carefully from tie to tie as I go back to Mom and Dusty in the shed. My eyes have stopped spinning but I keep my gaze fixed on the shed until I get there and open the door.

"So what do you think?" Dusty asks.

"That was great," I lie. "Thanks!"

2018

Golf

I walk through the dark culvert under the highway, the concrete ceiling just high enough to clear my head, the floor thick with greasy silt pocked by animal tracks, raccoons mostly although possums, skunks, and rats—plenty of rats—have been there, too. I can't see the light from the other end for a long time but it never gets completely black, not even dark enough to justify a flashlight, which I don't have anyway. I'm not scared now, but the first time I was. Then, fear made my knees weak and my neck sweaty and my breath come short as the light disappeared behind me. That time, I closed my mind to the possible horrors and forced myself forward. Now I do the same and tell myself I am not afraid. Soon I will be in the light.

The culvert burrows under tons of graded but not-yet-paved earth, the road bed that will become US 36, a four-lane highway plied by anonymous brontosauran trucks laden with cattle and grain and chemicals and industrial provender through the city to the bridge spanning the Missouri River. Where I walk beneath it, the dirt is piled forty feet or more above me, a mountain of earth held up by the thick concrete shell of the culvert. If I hold my hand against the ceiling, I imagine I can feel the immense weight of it. There is no sound from above; the newly-constructed highway isn't even paved yet. All I hear are my own heartbeats and a lot of little clawed feet scurrying ahead of me in the dark.

I press on, forcing my footsteps forward, more afraid of being afraid than of finding a creature waiting for me in the murk. Finally, the tunnel begins to brighten as each footstep carries me closer to daylight. The animal sounds disappear and whatever creature made them scrambles out the end before I can see it. I follow and take a huge breath of clean air and turn my face to the sunlight. After that first time, this time is easy.

The culvert opens next to Fairview Municipal Golf Course where I climb over the chain link fence and follow the creek that flows out of the culvert and across the course. I keep my eyes open: there are golf balls to be found. I keep them open, too, for the golf pro who runs the course. He'll confiscate any balls I find and run me off with threats to call the cops because I am trespassing.

I love rambling along the creek bank in the summer when the bullfrogs belly flop into the water as I get closer. I know where to turn over rocks to find crawdads, too. One way to catch them is to tie a bit of dead cricket to a string and let it drift under the rock. When they grab it with their pincers, you can pull them right out if you don't jerk it too fast. I don't know where I learned that trick, maybe from my father. The finest bird on the creek is the redwing blackbird that perches on the cattails swaying in the breeze.

Low dams make ponds at three places along the creek but they are too shallow for any fish bigger than minnows. I always thought minnows were just baby fish, but if that's what they are and the ponds are too shallow for grownup finners, how were they fathered? Maybe minnows aren't baby fish after all. Maybe they are just full-grown and tiny, flourishing where there are no bigger fish to eat them.

In the fall, the grass on the course turns pale sienna and washed-over gold. The reeds along the creek bank grow brittle and rattle in the chill breezes. Early morning frost sparkles in the sun and the grass crackles under my sneakers. Skins of ice lay over the quiet eddies of the creek and along the edges of the pond waiting for passing time to freeze over the whole of them when the winter comes on full. In that season, I leave footprints in the white rime but I don't worry about detection—the golf pro has gone south for the winter and few golfers face the cutting wind to play their game.

It is summer, so I follow the creek to the other side of the golf course where it disappears in another culvert, this one a corrugated metal tube just barely visible in the overgrowth surrounding its mouth. The tube carries the creek under the railroad grade that's been there much longer than the new highway. The tube under the railroad grade is round but tall enough to creep through if you duck. The bottom is flat, filled with silt that turns to gooey mud when rain raises the creek. Stalactites of black tar hang from the top like sticky spider threads that grab my hair unless I bend way over to avoid them. It's hard to walk that way for long, though, so I know I will get snagged by the tar someplace. The tube curves, so there is a stretch where light is blocked from both ends. The only way to get through without a flashlight is to trust my feet to stay out of the water in the center and to trail one hand along the tarred side to keep my balance and my bearings. The journey through is no adventure, it's simply a filthy trek. I don't like it so I only do it once just to overcome my fear and prove to myself I can.

I could retrace my steps through the tube to get back to the golf course, but it's nasty in there so I climb the face of the grade, push through the uncut weeds, work my way around the brambles and thorny briars until I get to the track bed on top. I know if I follow the tracks west I will come to the swing bridge over the river.

There's nothing to fear on the railroad tracks running along the golf course. Wide sky spreads above me, a small farm squats on the other side of the tracks, cinder ballast crunches beneath my feet. I walk east on the tracks balancing on the steel rail sometimes, other times trying to match my stride to the spacing of the wooden ties.

Just before I get to a cut where the tracks go through hills on both sides, I slip off onto a narrow trail, made by deer most likely, that leads back onto the golf course. I follow it up to the highest point on the course where I can see all the way to the clubhouse atop a far hill on the other side of the creek. The ponds glisten in the distance below, the whole picture framed by railroad tracks on one side and unfinished highway on the other. I stop to take it in while I catch my breath from the climb. I am the only human in the whole vista and I relish it.

A pear tree stands off the fairway in the rough where only the worst golfers hit their balls. Its fruit is sticky sweet and juicy at summer's end. I am lucky and find a pear hanging within reach just ready to drop, perfect in its not-yet-mushy ripeness. I pluck it from the branch, look it over closely for worm holes, then take a bite. The skin pops between my teeth and the syrupy nectar floods my tongue. I have to lean forward while I eat it to keep the sticky juice from running down my chin and dripping a glorious mess onto my tee shirt.

Later, the golf course provides another escape for me. I begin caddying when I am twelve, not long after we have moved to Jackson Street and I have discovered the culvert and Lou starts telling me I should earn my keep. A golfer I encounter on one of my course rambles offers me a dollar to carry his bag. He's almost done with his round but tired, so I pick up an easy buck and get hooked.

I show up at the clubhouse the next Saturday morning and ask the guy behind the counter if I can caddie. "Guess so," he says, then adds, "Good luck." I don't know what he means by that, but I hang out on a bench on the clubhouse porch all morning. No one hires me and I understand his comment. There aren't any other caddies, which should have tipped me off to my prospects. Fairview is a baked-out muni played mostly by blue collar retirees. I keep showing up, though, and asking the golfers as they walk by if they need a caddie and occasionally someone feeling flush or taking pity on me will give me a couple of dollars—literally—to haul their clubs up and down the hills.

After a month of this, a pair of my grandmother's tavern customers hear from her what I'm doing. They find me at the course and give me a permanent gig. Bill Betts and Norman (Nimmie) Sparger play every Saturday and Sunday morning before heading to the tavern. I carry for one or the other every weekend day. Two bucks a loop and they buy me a Coke at the turn. I have an income as long as it doesn't rain.

I also get an introduction to golf in the classic caddie way. Bill and Nimmie cobble together a set of old clubs and a ratty bag to get me started in the game. Bill isn't much of a golfer—he hits a big, looping slice on every shot—but Nimmie is a player. He has a flat, smooth swing that produces a running draw that plays beautifully on the hard un-watered fairways. His clubs are custom-made, too; built by Kenny Smith with fiberglass shafts, a crude precursor to the graphite composite wonders used today. Nimmie shows me how to grip a club and gives me a few pointers on how to swing it, but my ball flight resembles Bill's more than his.

Nimmie is a unique character. He is a retired meat cutter who lives with his aged mother and has never married. If he is gay, I don't detect it or even think of it, actually. He never makes any unwelcome gestures or suggestions to me, even when he takes me and another boy to Minnesota to go fishing. Nimmie doesn't drive, which makes him doubly unusual in St. Joseph. To get to Minnesota, we take a taxi from his house to the Greyhound terminal, then the bus to Minneapolis. I assume everything was arranged in advance, so I am surprised when we jump into a cab in Minneapolis and Nimmie asks the driver if he knows any good fishing camps. Off we go. Somehow, we end up with a cabin on a lake, a row boat, and enough groceries to last a week. Because we have no car, we are stranded there until the cabbie comes back to get us. We fish, eat what we catch, then fish some more. I am thirteen and Jimmy, the boy who caddied for Nimmie before me, is fourteen or so.

Caddying is hard work when the golf bag full of clubs and gear weighs almost as much as you do and the course is built on three unrelenting hills. I handle it, though, learning to sling the bag across my back so the weight rests on my hips and not my shoulders. My second year, I splurge on a pair of leather golf shoes. They give my feet a lot more support that the Keds that I wear every day and the metal spikes provide extra traction on the hillsides. They also make a crisp, masculine crunch on the concrete sidewalk in front of the clubhouse that announces serious golfers are walking here.

Nimmie teaches me how to tend the flag, fix a ball mark on the green, replace a divot, rake a bunker. I learn to mentally link where the ball lands with a landmark like a tree or bush so I can find it in the rough if necessary. When my player is hitting, I stand slightly aside from face-on to him, never behind his back or on the path of his backswing. It's simple stuff and mostly common sense, but an essential part of the game.

Even lugging a bag, I love walking the course. I smell fresh grass and musky leaf litter under the trees. Wind kisses my cheeks and flicks the cattails in the creek. Even when the sun glares, it cleans and brightens everything it touches while darkening the shade under the trees for contrast. I am alive and notice everything from the tiny spike mark on the tee box to the fairway's march uphill to a flagstick silhouetted against clouds on the horizon.

With Jim (Beau) Lyons at Bethpage Black c 2014

With my first car, a 1955 Chevy, 1967

High School

The first class on my first day in high school was Latin, which I had chosen because, to my freshman ego, it sounded more intellectual than French or Spanish, the other two languages offered. At that time, a year of foreign language study was required for graduation. That day was also the first one on the job for our newly-minted teacher, a skinny, sweet-faced, dishwater blonde who didn't look much older than her students and who arrived in the classroom late, slightly disheveled, and carrying a motorcycle helmet. She's kind of cute, I thought. Maybe high school is going to be fun.

And it turned out to be just that. Those four years were among the best in my life, full of achievements and stupid stunts, memorable teachers and forgettable classwork, awards, jobs, girlfriends, parties, cars, beer, music, and friendships made that lasted our lifetimes. I blossomed in high school. I learned to juggle multiple responsibilities as editor of the school paper, student director of the all-school play, member of the student council cabinet, debate team, chess club, and various other nerdy pursuits—all while working in a gas station after school and weekends, teaching myself to play the guitar, and hanging out with my friends. It was a glorious time.

I also got a taste of leadership and learned to enjoy the spotlight that came with it. Good grades often got me noticed in class and my readiness and ability to speak out reinforced my position. When something needed to be done, teachers tended to turn to me and so did my classmates once they found out I accepted almost any responsibility. Academics aside, high school taught me many valuable lessons, most of them about myself and my capabilities.

Our earnest and sweetly naïve freshman Latin teacher tried to interest us in the subject by showing us how the Romans lived and what they created. Along with conjugating *amo, amas, amat,* we created homemade displays along the order of Roman-themed science projects. I built a foot-long model of a trireme that was remarkable in its detail--the carving of all those individual oars was a chore--and also for its triangular hull, a feature made necessary by my inability to bend the balsa wood to an authentic curved shape.

Second-year Latin was taught in a more conventional way by a cheerful veteran whose neatly curled gray hair denoted her years of explaining the significance of *veni, vedi, vici* to dis-interested sophomores. In the spring, she took over the Latin I class in addition to her own when our freshman teacher broke her leg in a motorcycle accident. I never heard how it happened, but I'm sure the details weren't nearly as scandalous as I imagined them.

Latin class was the natural habitat of the nerds, or the "intelligentsia," as we preferred to call ourselves. That first day I noticed a tall, sloppy kid slouched at his desk doodling in his notebook. His name was Steve Smith and he was drawing one of the intricate, outrageous cartoons that would eventually get us both in various kinds of hot water. Steve was one of the first of us to get a car by virtue of his early birth date. He bought a rust-bucket Rambler, once forest green, now faded to khaki, with a label he glued on the glove box that said "Do Not Feed the Oogantetherium." To Steve's credit, he refused to explain the phrase. He was one of the groom's men at my first wedding and went with us when I took Jeremy to see *Star Wars* when it came out. Steve went into the army after college but we kept in touch through long, absurd letters until our lives finally diverged.

The other Smith I met in high school was Daniel F., son of upper middle class parents, smarter than his achievements showed, and as easy-going as a product tester in a La-Z-Boy factory. If it felt good, Dan did it—as long as it required no extra effort. When he went to college, popular opinion held that he would never graduate but instead become the world's oldest living undergrad, perpetually just one term paper short of earning a degree. He proved us wrong, but just barely.

Dan and I were co-editors of the school paper, a position that suited his talents perfectly. It came out every two weeks, so there wasn't much to the job until the night before deadline, when we had to buckle down. We were experts at that rhythm of work, he and I, and made a perfect team. Dan would stand by while I did most of the work, which suited me fine since I always wanted to be in charge. We put our method to good use once to write a team term paper for one of our senior year social studies classes. Our chosen subject was drug use in the student body at Central High—actually a pretty hot topic for the mid-sixties. As usual, we didn't do any work until the night before the paper was due. Dan and I holed up in my room with my second-hand typewriter and knocked out fifteen pages of pure fiction on the subject. We based our "analysis" on invented interviews with anonymous sources and reports of purely-imaginary personal observations of pot parties and drug sales on campus. It was a work of art that earned us an "A."

It also earned us a summons to the principal's office. Mr. Baker, the principal, was disturbed by the sordid picture we had painted of his school and wanted the identities of our anonymous "sources" as well as the students we had "witnessed" selling and buying drugs. Dan and I looked at each other. He shrugged, leaving the solution to me.

"We can't do that, Mr. Baker," I said in as level a tone as I could muster. "We promised them we wouldn't use their names and we can't go back on our word."

He harangued us for a while, threatened to tell our parents, suspend us, even to turn the paper over to the police, but we stood our ground. We were outwardly respectful and polite, but we didn't give an inch. Finally, he either decided we really were not going to rat on our sources or that parental and/or police involvement would generate too much bad publicity. Regardless, he let us go, threatening that he would keep an eye on us. He also warned us to stay clear of the drug users in school. With great solemnity, we assured him we would.

Later that year, Dan and I were back in Mr. Baker's office facing another threat to our journalistic integrity--only this one was legitimate. We had used our positions as editors of the *Outlook,* the school newspaper, to minimize its coverage of trifles like the results of cheerleading tryouts and French club elections in order to make room for articles and editorials on student protests across the nation and the defining topics of our generation, the civil rights movement and the Vietnam war. The fact that Central High School and indeed, St. Joseph itself, were oblivious to those issues didn't matter to us. It was our duty as journalists to bring them to the attention of the student body whether they wanted to read such news or not.

Our reportage was only the spark that fired Mr. Baker's tinder, however. It was the other Smith's work—Steve Smith—that poured gasoline on the flame. He drew and we published a series of bizarre, vaguely anti-establishment cartoons that even Steve had difficulty explaining. What was clear in each, however, were his initials, "S.D.S." Someone, a concerned school board member perhaps, noticed this lettering in the cartoon and decided it was the acronym for one of the leading radical groups of the day, "Students for a Democratic Society."

Mr. Baker was somewhat flummoxed by my explanation that "SDS" stood for "Steven Dennis Smith" but gathered his wits finally and pointed out that we had given the school a black eye with our whole editorial slant. That's a good sign, I thought; we finally got somebody's attention. Then he added that we had also sullied the reputation of Florence McCoy, our journalism teacher and staff sponsor of the newspaper, and that some members of the school board were making ugly threats. We didn't know if he was bluffing or not, but I didn't feel so good about that. Mrs. McCoy was a sweet, innocent person who bore no culpability for our actions. When I protested that the newspaper's content was our responsibility and protected by the First Amendment, Baker's response set me back for a minute.

"The school pays for it, the printing and everything," he said, "and Mrs. McCoy is the faculty sponsor, so it reflects on all of us." Then a light bulb came on in his head. "Here's what's going to happen if you publish any more of this Commie garbage: You're going to pay for it. I'll send a bill to your parents." I am sure he thought he had us there. Again, Dan and I exchanged looks. Parental involvement didn't concern us in the least. If it actually happened, Dan's father would just write a check and Lou would make me pay and I didn't have any money. Dan shrugged as usual.

"Okay," I said, perhaps too readily.

"And I want to see the next issue before it goes to press," Baker added.

"Yes, sir," Dan said.

Exasperated but sensing a win, Baker waved us out of his office. We hung our heads until we got into the hall. Then Dan slapped me on the back. The school year was ending and there were no more issues of the *Outlook* to be printed anyway.

VFW Voice of Democracy, 1968

Speaking

I stand before the microphone in a hotel banquet room full of businessmen. I am only a little afraid, but that is good because the adrenaline in my bloodstream will give my speech a shot of extra energy. I swim in these waters like a marlin, strong, alert, and confident in my abilities. This Optimist Club speech contest doesn't daunt me—I've competed and won in dozens just like it, many times in front of much larger and tougher audiences than this gathering of local shopkeepers and insurance agents.

Gathering my breath to begin with power, I survey the crowd and detect a fleeting smirk on one of the well-fed faces. It seems to say, who does this scrawny sixteen-year-old think he is? I am suddenly conscious of my thrift-shop blazer and Sears and Roebuck tie, the loose fit of the hand-me-down shirt my Mom ironed fresh this morning, the run-down heels of my penny loafers, scuffed and dull despite the polish I applied last night. Through force of will, I push the doubt down inside my core and smile at the audience. I begin my speech sure I will win.

After all, I have defeated this particular opponent before. He is Davis Martin, the boy with two first names as we called him, and he doesn't compete often. When he does, he speaks through tightly pursed lips like a caricature of some Connecticut preppie. His diction is indistinct, his cadence clipped as if he can't be bothered to enunciate clearly or complete his sentences so his listeners can comprehend what he's saying. He deigns to speak to people below his station only because he can't avoid them entirely. I glance at him as I begin my second paragraph. The shopkeeper I spotted earlier may not have been smirking, but Davis is.

I first met Davis in freshman Latin and it didn't take me long to figure out he didn't just come from the opposite side of the tracks from me, he descended from a distant planet. Davis arrived on his first day in high school dressed in gray flannel slacks, tassel loafers, bone-white shirt with French cuffs complete with gold links, and a navy blazer sporting a silk pocket square. All he lacked was an Ascot – and I suspect he had taken that off just before entering the classroom. You might have thought he was trying to impress someone, but no, that was just him. He stayed that way throughout our four years in high school.

Against a phony like that, how can I not win this simple service club speech contest?

Several excellent teachers have made a winning competitive speaker out of me. Colleen Chronister, who taught English and drama and masterminded the all-school play, showed me how to turn stage fright into stage energy and how to not fear looking foolish while projecting emotion through dramatic gestures, facial expression, and vocal gymnastics. Marsha Eichenberg, our speech teacher, introduced me to the intellectual pugilism that is competitive debate. Dick and I signed up for the debate team as soon as it was formed and competed together for three glorious seasons. The research skills, the disciplined analytic thinking and the rigorous concentration during competition proved useful to me the rest of my life. Dick and I win more than our fair share of debates in tournaments against other schools in the region. In addition, I compete in other events like individual oratory, poetry recitation, and extemporaneous speaking, where contestants are assigned a previously-unannounced topic to expound on after only a few minutes of preparation. I also take on impromptu speaking, where you have less than a minute to prepare before delivering a talk on a blindly-drawn topic. Only the fearless succeed in that event where projected confidence wins over thoughtful verbiage every time.

I discover through speaking that I crave not attention but acclaim. I don't really get much of a charge from standing in front of an audience, but I absolutely love their ovations. The applause of the crowd, the awards and prizes I earn, the praise from my teachers, teammates, and friends all fill a void in me that I didn't know I had until the hands started clapping. I don't recognize it at the time, but I will strive to earn such accolades throughout my life.

My greatest triumph in high school was the Veterans of Foreign Wars *Voice of Democracy* contest, which came the year before this Optimist Club event. The VFW contest was one of the easiest I ever entered. After weeks of honing my speech and performance under Mrs. Chronister's demanding tutelage, I delivered it in one take in an audio recording booth at KFEQ Radio with a sound engineer as my only audience. I guess that could be considered the first step in what would be my long career in broadcasting. The tape went on to be judged at various levels until months later when it won the Missouri state competition. In addition to a $500 savings bond, I won a trip to Washington, DC, where the other state winners and I would see the capital and a national champion would be chosen.

The world opened to me when I won that contest. I relished the stories in the local press and became a minor celebrity in school. I was invited to deliver the speech to local service clubs, at the Missouri VFW convention in Joplin, and at a Fourth of July celebration in front of a vast crowd at Kansas City's Liberty Memorial. The cherry on top, though, came when I boarded a

TWA 707 at Kansas City's Municipal Airport for my first ride on a plane. I didn't win the national contest, but the honor of the trip itself provided memories that bucked me up throughout my life. Even today, one of the ways I fight depression and disappointment is to mentally relive that small-scale triumph.

I kept a treacly journal devoted to my impressions on the trip. It detailed the historical shrines we visited, many of which moved me deeply, and the political dignitaries we met, nearly all of whom disgusted me. It was 1968, a turbulent election year, and the contest was part of the VFW national convention, a huge gathering that attracted politicians like cockroaches drawn to sugar spilled on the kitchen counter.

One of them was True Davis, a relative to my Optimist Club opponent. True was a former ambassador to Switzerland, president of a Washington bank, and a man about town in the nation's capital. Many years later in the small world department, my mom cleaned the Davis McMansion for a few years.

But now Davis and I face off in front of the local Optimist Club. I finish my speech, pause to receive a round of polite applause, and sit down to listen to Davis. The man who had smirked at me smiles broadly as Davis approaches the podium. So does the man seated next to him. Davis mumbles through his presentation, the crowd applauds long and hard, and we are asked to leave the room while they chose a winner. It doesn't take long.

Second prize is a nicely printed certificate suitable for framing as long as the frame is equally disposable. Receiving it doesn't hurt me as much as watching Davis accept the $100 savings bond for first place. I need that money a whole lot more than he does—and I deserve it more, too.

With Grandma (Cecile) Russell, 1952

House on Jackson Street

Work

When I was twelve, like most people at any age, money was my primary motivation for working. There were other reasons then (and certainly now), but mostly, I needed the cash. I never received an allowance and wasn't paid for household chores like emptying the trash and raking the leaves. When it came to giving me an allowance, Mom didn't have any money even after she married Lou. He gave her money to buy food and pay the household bills, but spent any extra on his cars and his garage. We weren't exactly poor, but we were sure frugal. Mom bought our clothes with the pittance of household money he gave her, which is probably why we were always grateful to receive a box of hand-me-downs from Aunt Cecile, whose three sons were older and larger than me but wore clothes I could eventually kind of grow into. The cast-offs weren't rags; Cecile could afford quality because Uncle Hank was a Lt. Colonel in the Air Force and they lived accordingly well, at least in comparison to us. Still, it was fortunate for me that the style of the day included jeans with rolled-up cuffs.

As far as Lou was concerned, my chores around the house were a fair trade for meals Mom fed me with food he'd paid for and the roof over my head he provided. Want a couple of dollars for a model car? I knew better than to ask because I knew the answer: go find a job. He never missed a chance to harp about it, either. My lack of a job—before I could even drive— was a frequent topic at the dinner table and, if he saw me with my nose in a book during the day, he would point out that nobody ever got paid for reading.

One day, Mom interrupted one of his harangues to offer a suggestion. "David," she said, "why don't you mow some lawns around the neighborhood? You could earn some money that way."

Before I could answer, Lou jumped in. "You have to buy your own gas," he said. "And who's going to pay for the wear and tear on my lawn mower?" I guess I could have offered him a cut of my yet-unearned income, but I didn't answer. What do you say to a bully like that?

Eventually, I more or less worked seven days a week, including holidays, because Lou had dirty jobs he wanted done and, at my age, I was cheap, available labor for his garage behind the house where he did auto body repair and painting. Some of the cars belonged to friends of his, others were repossessed cars sent by a bank loan officer that was a friend of Mom's from high school. On days when I wasn't caddying, my job was to wet-sand the cars in preparation for painting. It was messy, monotonous work done entirely by hand using 400-grit sandpaper and a sponge dripping water onto the surface for lubrication. Eight hours of pushing that sandpaper was filthy and brutal. At first, Lou expected me to work for nothing just like I did around the house. When Mom found out, she protested and he gave me a whopping dollar an hour. I guess I was supposed to feel grateful for the money, but the job mainly taught me to hate cars about as much as I hate snow. Lou used all the cheap labor he could get in the garage. Along with bodywork, he detailed the repos for the bank, which was gnarly work. I did some of it, but he mostly pressed Mom into the job for the interiors. Every surface inside, from the headliner to under the seats and inside the trunk, had to be vacuumed and shampooed. Dashboards were cleaned with toothbrushes. You'd think they were show cars the way he insisted on perfection. It didn't do Mom's back any good, either, since she had to twist around and bend to reach every crease and corner.

After school let out the summer I turned sixteen, I stopped caddying to work in a gas station on the weekends and got a back-breaking Monday through Friday job mowing grass at the East Hills Shopping Center. The entire periphery of the parking lot was a strip of grass, almost all of it on a grade that was too steep for a riding mower or tractor. It was just fine for a push mower propelled by a ninety-pound boy, however, as long as he paid attention to the slope and didn't slip on the freshly-mowed grass and cut off his foot. It took a week of eight hour days to shove that mower around the entire property. Then I started over. The Missouri humidity was brutal and the sun was damn hot. The stink and clatter of the two-cycle engine amplified the misery. Muscling that clunky mower sideways along the grade took the pluck right out of me. No matter how tired I was, though, I had to keep pushing at a steady pace because getting the mower moving from a full stop on the hillside took extra energy I didn't have. At the end of the day, I was covered in sweat and grass clippings, my sneakers and blue jeans stained green, my eyes red from the glare of the sun and the fumes of the mower exhaust.

Why did I do it? It wasn't the meager paycheck, although I wanted it. The job paid the same as Lou—and taxes were taken out of that. I did it because it beat sanding cars and I wasn't working for Lou when I reported to my job at the shopping center. Besides, it was the only full-time job I could find at my age. You had to have a job in Lou's house. If you didn't, you were a bum; you were nothing. The job didn't matter as long as you got paid for doing it.

The mowing job ended when school started but I still worked in the gas station after school and on weekends. A schedule like that wouldn't work for a lot of kids, but I had no problem because I didn't need to study much and what little homework I absolutely had to do I could finish at night after I got home or during the quiet of Sunday afternoons in the gas station. I cut out most after-school activities, but that didn't bother me since I wasn't part of the social crowd at school anyway. Besides, I had to work.

It was in the Mobil station at 22nd and Frederick that I developed my life-long hatred of snow. Lou had worked there at one time and lined up the job for me. The owner had a contract with a telephone company garage around the corner that kept the station alive. The linemen and their trucks came in every day for gas since they needed to keep their tanks full in case of emergencies. We also serviced those trucks, changing the oil and filters, lubricating joints with a grease gun, checking belts, lights, and fluids every month and hand-washing them every Saturday.

The real fun came when it snowed. As the first flakes fell, the trucks lined up so we could put chains on their rear tires. We'd pull a truck into a bay, slip a pneumatic jack under the rear bumper to lift both tires at the same time, then another guy and I would roll under those tires on a creeper so the chains could be fastened on both the outer and the inner, or axle side, of the tires. The whole process took probably five minutes. The ugly part came when it had to be done in reverse once the snow stopped. Each truck pulled into the bay, the pneumatic jack lifted up its rear end, and I again had to slide under the tires to release the chains. Only now the entire underside of the truck was caked with a nasty mixture of melting snow, ice, dirt, and road salt that glopped repeatedly into my face. Thirty sets of chains every time it snowed. When it snows today, I can taste that glop on my lips.

Years later, I was telling my friend Dick once about how lucky I felt to have the things I had—a good wife, great kids, a nice home, money in the bank. I'd been able to travel much of the world, indulge my passions for golf, music, photography, and woodworking, and my retirement was pretty much secured at an early point in my financial life. "Lucky," I said.

"Captain," Dick replied, "You're the hardest working son-of-a-bitch I know. You earned every bit of your luck."

On reflection, I guess he was right. And maybe I should thank Lou for some of my "luck." His tight-fisted ways showed me how miserable life without money could be and his constant carping about my lack of a job motivated me to go find one if for no other reason than to shut him up about it. Apparently, even a bully can do some unintentional good. Until I got into broadcasting, most of my jobs were pretty miserable ones. I learned some valuable lessons, though, even if I didn't recognize them at the time. I learned how to turn my mind to something else while my body focused on the drudgery at hand. I also learned that, no matter how tiring and mindless a job may be, every shift eventually ends and the way to get to the end is to just keep pushing that sandpaper.

Today, work is a sacrament to me. It contradicts a cliché to say so, but I believe work defines a person. Unfortunately, many people confuse their job with their work. Your job is where you go to earn some money. It's what Lou forced me to do. Your work, though, is the effort you put into accomplishing worthwhile things in life and it may or may not involve a paycheck. Sometimes you are fortunate and your job enables you to do your chosen work; other times, it seems to stand in the way of it and can't be avoided since you have to keep body and soul together. If you are mentally strong enough, though, even the most menial of jobs can become fulfilling work that provides a sense of accomplishment. Did I make the world a better place by mowing all that grass every week? No. Did I finish the task and do it well? You bet.

With Mom and Jeremy on his
Great-grandmother Russell's lap, 1974

Robbed

Jere Loyd and I got close in junior high where he, Dick, and I formed sort of a triumvirate of nerds. Later, in high school, Jere was also my supervisor when I got robbed.

Jere was and is a stalwart person, a guy you can always trust to do the right thing, to stand by his word and take his responsibilities to heart. That's why the owner of the two Clark Super 100 gas stations in town made him a manager at the young age of sixteen. Jere pretty much ran the station on Mitchell Avenue and recommended me for a job pumping gas on weekends at the other one, which was located at the corner of Frederick Boulevard and 22nd Street, next door to the fire house where Lou worked and across the street from the Mobil station where I would work after the robbery.

When I got the job, I was a few weeks short of being old enough to drive, so Mom chauffeured me to and from work just as she did to the shopping center to mow the grass during the week. She was driving my car, the 1955 Chevy I bought for $50 after making a deal with Lou that she could drive it until I got my license. As part of the deal, Lou would pay the insurance while she used the car. He would also help fix it up with me doing the grunt work and paying for all the parts. That actually was pretty generous on his part since, among other things, the engine needed a major overhaul, the transmission had to be replaced, and the last owner had painted one fender with a brush. I couldn't deal with those problems myself nor could I afford to pay garage rates to have the work done.

James Dean wouldn't be caught dead in my Chevy. It had a reliable but very unsexy 135 horsepower 235 cubic inch in-line six-cylinder engine and a three-speed manual transmission with a not-snazzy shifter on the steering column. Given my lack of budget for upgrades, there was no V-8 with four-on-the floor in my future. But Lou shaved most of the chrome trim off its body to make it sleeker and painted it all over a jazzy pearl blue. I couldn't afford chrome wheels, but black rims with baby moon hubcaps added a custom touch. Seat covers (not expensive re-upholstery) made it respectable. I had turned sixteen and been driving the Chevy to work myself just a couple of weeks before I got robbed.

The Clark station had a few gas pumps but no service bays, only a glass-enclosed office with a back room where motor oil was stacked and cartons of cigarettes were stored in a padlocked plywood cabinet. The cabinet also held a leather pouch where the attendant on duty—me—stashed the cash receipts as they came in. I wore white pinstriped coveralls with a chrome coin dispenser on my belt and carried a leather wallet chained to the belt as well. I made change for customers from there and periodically put the overflow into the cabinet for safe keeping. I was very conscientious about it, since the owner's policy regarding shortages was simple: employees had to make up any shortfall from their shift. You signed for the petty cash, cigarette inventory, and pump readings when you came on duty, then repeated the process at the end. If the receipts didn't cover the sales, the difference came out of your pocket. It was not only a surefire way to eliminate employee theft, but basically insured the owner against losses by shifting the risk to his employees. I'm not sure it was legal, but I am certain it was good for him and bad for us.

The crime itself didn't generate any headlines. The day of the robbery was sunny and warm, a slow, summer afternoon. On weekend days like that there wasn't much to do around the station once the trash on the lot was swept up and the bathrooms were cleaned. When business was really slow and I had nothing to read, I passed the time by smashing flies against the windows by snapping them with a rolled-up towel. Entertaining in a sad way, and also messy—the windows had to be cleaned of all the dead fly splats before the shift ended.

I sat staring into space doing nothing when a non-descript car pulled up to a pump and the driver told me to fill it up. He and a passenger got out and asked for the restroom so I told them where to find the key hanging in the glass-enclosed office. I started the gas flowing into his tank and began wiping the windshield. Clean windows and an offer to check the oil were part of my job description.

As I worked my way around the car rubbing the windows with a clean cloth, I discovered a very interesting girl about my age curled up in the back seat. As I went from window to window, she stretched like a cat awakening from a nap. She raised her arms languorously and her tee shirt slid up to expose a cute little navel peeking above denim shorts that were unbuttoned at the top. She smiled at me through the back window while pulling the shirt up just a bit more to reveal a sliver of the bottom of her bra. I grinned back as the gas pump clanged its shut-off signal and the driver and passenger came back to the car.

The driver handed me a twenty dollar bill, then tried to pull a quick change switch trick that I'd seen before. I kept my wits about me and gave him the correct change, feeling pretty smart about beating the con game. When he got back in the car and drove away, the girl in the back set sat up and looked back at me, expressionless. I was too suave to wave even though I really wanted to. Another car pulled up to a pump. It was several minutes before I went into the back room to deposit the cash from the recent sales. The plywood cabinet door had been jimmied open, the padlock dangled from the latch, the cash pouch was gone.

I called Jere and he called the cops, but it was a futile effort since I couldn't even tell them what make or even color the car was, much less the license number. All I could remember was the girl's smooth belly with its cute little navel, which I didn't report, and the failed short con, which I did. "Just grifters passing through," the cops said. "They'll never be found."

Jere tried to stand up for me, but the owner wasn't having any of it. I had to pay back what amounted to a full shift's receipts. I worked without pay for three weeks. At $1.15 an hour, it took that long to accumulate the stolen money. Then I quit. I sometimes wonder what would have happened if I'd simply refused to work it off and quit the job, but that didn't seem to be an option at the time. I also wonder what ever became of that girl with the cute navel.

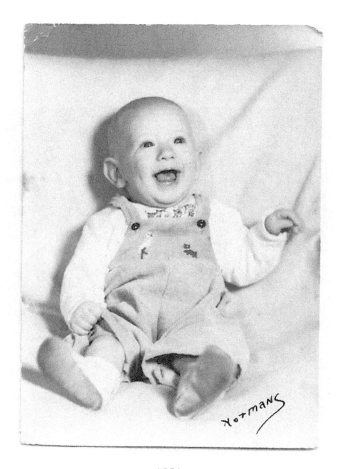

1951

Sarah and Jasper Welch (my great-great-grandparents) and family. Josie Mae (my great-grandmother) 2nd from left rear

Politics

Successful politicians are the ones who have perfected the art of swindling shallow thinkers into giving their votes and donations to someone who mouths the clichés they want to hear and displays the attitude they want to see. It matters not if the candidate intends to deliver on promises made, just that the voter hears what he or she wants to hear. The goal of the politician is not public service; it is power to grab financial gain and insure job security. A really effective politician will not only live well while in office but have a cushy job waiting with a major donor when they finally step down, lose an election, or get out of jail. Performance and civic achievement for the common good matter naught. What counts is accumulating more votes than the next guy and that is done by astute message control. Find out which way the wind is blowing and aim your hot air in the same direction. The mob rules; all you have to do is seem to be at its forefront while traveling in the direction it wants to go.

My political opinions have changed over time although they went in the opposite direction from the norm, from right to left instead of the usual knee-jerk-liberal to old-geezer-conservative. My family was traditionally Republican—Grandma had a collection of glass elephants, which gives you some idea of our leanings. But identifying as a Republican in those days didn't mean you were necessarily a hard-boiled right winger. When I was a toddler, President Ike was grandfather to us all and I cared not (nor knew) what policies he favored.

John Kennedy was the first president whose beliefs and activities made an impression on me. I vividly recall his leadership during the hysteria surrounding the Russian missiles in Cuba and the duck and cover drills that were supposed to save our young lives when the nuclear warheads came flying from across the sea. If I had known how severe the crisis really was, I probably would have been scarred for life.

Not long after Kennedy was assassinated, I became a political creature. Not that his death had anything to do with it other than it brought Lyndon Johnson into the White House and Johnson's public persona struck me as unworthy of the office. I couldn't tell you what he stood for, only that he was a redneck buffoon.

By 1964, my guy was Barry Goldwater. His ideas were so clear cut and simple I couldn't understand why everyone didn't immediately see how valid they were. He was also the underdog, which automatically raised him several notches in my esteem. If I were going to campaign for someone, it had to be for the least popular figure. I was thirteen when I read his book, *Conscience of a Conservative*, and it sold me on him completely. I don't know how I came to have a copy, but I probably picked it up at a campaign event because it was free. I even volunteered to go door to door passing out literature for Barry, a task made more enjoyable by doing it in the company of Dick and Jere, not to mention a shapely young lady who made up the other member of our campaign team.

Despite our noble efforts, of course, Goldwater went down in flames ignited by the infamous mushroom cloud TV commercial. A couple of years later, my right wing mindset found an outlet in the Young Americans for

Freedom, which was run locally by a couple of junior college students who appreciated my virulent anti-Communism and my ardor for black and white solutions to America's problems. "Better dead than red" was my motto, although that would change as the probability of going to Vietnam increased a couple of years later. YAF was organized and purposeful, though, and completely contrary to the image of youth projected by the media of the day. Contrarian to the bone, I had found my niche. I also found myself in charge of the chapter as the older members went off to college.

Not content to meet among ourselves and preach to the choir, our tiny group cast about for some actions we could take to advance our cause on the battlefields of public opinion in St. Joseph. A local businessman gave us some money to educate the populace, so we brought in a Taiwanese author to lecture about the horrors of Mao Zedong and the dire need for the US to immediately go to war to restore Chiang Kai-Shek to power on the Chinese mainland, a cause that had been abandoned twenty years earlier by everyone except the John Birch Society. I had the honor of picking up our speaker at the airport in Kansas City and showing him around town. He was immensely interested in the Jesse James cabin. The scant dozen people who showed up to hear him speak nodded agreeably throughout his presentation but were not inspired to take up arms against Red China.

A few months later, the small but dedicated YAF membership took a cue from the left-wingers we saw on TV and mounted a protest march. Our cause? To stop IBM from supplying computers to the godless communists in Russia. Three of us walked in circles outside the local IBM office products store carrying hand-lettered signs and waving to the passing cars downtown. We didn't make any headlines, though, and the poor misguided commie symp inside the office didn't have a clue as to why we were there since his principal line of work was selling typewriters to lawyers, realtors, and banks, not missile guidance computer systems to the Kremlin.

When Richard Nixon ran for president in 1968, YAF morphed into the Young Republicans and I found myself the chairman of the Sixth Congressional District chapter of that upstanding youth organization. There were maybe six of us in the club. By that time, the Vietnam War was ramping up and registration for the draft was looming over me. My politics were changing, too, but Nixon said he had a secret plan to end the war. Enough said. He was the man who was going to keep me from dying in Vietnam.

Nixon never came to St. Joseph to campaign, but his running mate Spiro Agnew did. I picked up some of his entourage at the airport and drove them to a local rally. I never got to meet the great man himself, but I was part of his team, which was gratifying.

When the Nixon daughters came to Kansas City, Jere and I skipped school to join the crowd. I was smitten by Tricia Nixon. Her sister, Julie, the poor thing, looked a lot like her swarthy, jowly father. Tricia, though, had golden hair and a pert nose and carried herself like royalty. Jere and I worked our way through the crowd to get a better view as the girls mounted the stage. Tricia was as pretty up close as she was in the newspapers.

By the time she married Chris Cox, though, I was done with the whole lot of them. Nixon's big secret plan turned out to consist of bombing the hell out of Southeast Asia to pile more American and Vietnamese bodies on the funeral pyres. I had friends of friends who served in Vietnam and came back to report how fruitless it all was. Even my Uncle Hank, a career Air Force pilot who flew bombing missions during the war, was disillusioned by the futility of the effort. I couldn't vote in 1968, but when I did become old enough, I marked my first ballot in 1972 for George McGovern and never looked back at my right-wing Republican past.

At dedication of Harrison Public Library renovation, 2015

Leigh Anna's first birthday, 1978

Fatherhood

With Lois Green and Matt Cates, MWSC, 1970

Fatherhood

With Lois Green and Matt Cates, MWSC, 1970

College & Marriage

If it hadn't been for the Vietnam War, I never would have gone to college.

It was not so much that I didn't want to go, it's that I didn't know how to get there. I also lacked the help I needed to figure it out. I was a National Merit Scholar, but I didn't know what that meant besides getting my name in the paper. My high school counselor, a beleaguered woman who had some 450 other seniors to usher through the process, didn't notice my lack of college applications and I certainly didn't know where to begin the process on my own.

Mom and Lou had dropped out of high school themselves, and they saw college as something for rich kids. In their world, you got a job as soon as you were old enough, and that was that. Besides, college was expensive. I had no money nor any idea of how to go about applying for scholarships or loans. You might as well have asked me to draw the blueprints for a three-stage rocket.

So I graduated from high school and settled down to working in the gas station, playing my guitar, dating girls, and drinking beer. Sometime in the hazy future, I would write the great American novel—which I was sure didn't require a college education. All my friends were getting ready to leave for distant campuses and lives in dorms and frat houses and have experiences I couldn't even visualize. It didn't much bother me. They had their lots in life and I had mine, a modest one, and it was all I should expect given our low rung on society's ladder. I wasn't happy about it, but I wasn't crying into my pillow every night either.

What finally got me moving in the direction of college was the very real prospect of being sent to fight Lyndon Johnson's war. When I turned 18 that mid-summer, I received notice to register for the draft. It was 1969, the war was destroying our country along with Vietnam, and the prospect of being sent to Southeast Asia scared the hell out of me. I was dead set against the war – I even campaigned for Nixon in '68 based on his promise of a "secret plan" to end it – but I was even more dead set against getting killed. Short of enlisting, I didn't have a lot of choices. I could defect to Canada, which I couldn't begin to figure out how to do, get married and have a kid right away, which somehow seemed totally ill-advised, or go to college and get a student deferment. It was July by then, though, so it was way too late to apply most places even if I'd known how to go about it. That's how I ended up at Missouri Western College.

The school was opening on its new campus and enrolling its first four-year students. Until then, it had operated as St. Joseph Junior College, a two year community college that awarded associate degrees to kids who lacked the money, smarts, or ambition to get into a four-year college. The state of Missouri wanted to expand higher education, though, so it authorized and financed development of the school as a four-year institution. Best of all for me there wasn't exactly a waiting list to get in and, at $15 per credit hour, I could afford at least the first semester's tuition. I could live at home, keep my job in the gas station, and stay out of Vietnam.

As it turned out, I got a pretty good education at Missouri Western once I got there. My diploma might not open as many doors as one from Harvard or jump-start a career in investment banking, law, or medicine, but I learned to think critically, express myself clearly, and explore the world of ideas. I ran into some talented, devoted teachers who pushed me as far and as fast as I could go. Most of them were young and perhaps lacked credentials, ambition, or connections to get jobs at more prestigious schools, but they cared about their students.

One that stood out was Paula Vehlow, an English instructor. In the rush to register and my ignorance of the process, I somehow managed to get placed in a remedial English class despite my near-perfect high school transcript. It was a strange environment for me, to say the least. I couldn't figure out why—in college—the teacher had to explain to the students what a sentence was. And where to place the period. This went on for several weeks and my frustrations grew and grew. I finally wrote a particularly sarcastic passage in an assignment about paragraphs and Mrs. Vehlow called me into her office.

That was when I discovered that I was not in the advanced composition class I thought I'd signed up for. It was also when she and I learned it was too late to transfer. I needed an English credit, though, and my choices weren't pretty: I could drop the current class and wait until the next semester to get the advanced class I wanted, but that would put an "incomplete" on my transcript which might affect my student deferment. Or I could stay where I was and go insane. Mrs. Vehlow suggested an alternative. She would give me assignments and tutor me individually while I stayed enrolled in the class. She sure didn't have to do that and I sure didn't have to think twice before agreeing to it.

Her criticism of my work was pointed and unsparing and always fair. It is bracing to have someone dissect your thought processes as well as your prose the way she did it. She taught me how clear, accurate expression comes from clear, accurate ideas. The opposite is also true, of course. If the writing is muddy, generalized, or weaselly, the underlying thoughts are the same. I wish I could say I always achieved the clarity she preached. She also gave me at least a hundred books, most of them anthologies and advanced text books in composition and criticism that she received as samples. I still have dozens of them. Paula Vehlow was one of the most dedicated educators I've ever known.

The same couldn't be said of the instructor in the only class I ever failed. It was Art History, again a class I was in because the one I wanted—Art Appreciation—was full by the time I registered. Actually, I looked forward to the supposedly more advanced class, so I entered it with few regrets. Those came later.

I've blocked the instructor's cursed name from my memory, but I unabashedly blame him for the blot on my record that prevented my *cum laude* award when I graduated. The first session of the course set the debacle in motion. The instructor asked if everyone had purchased the absurdly expensive text book, then passed out a semester's worth of reading assignments in it. They started on page one and went straight through to the middle of the book, where the next semester's class would begin. After every few chapters were completed, tests were scheduled. Fair enough, I thought.

After the syllabus had been distributed, he darkened the room and started his lecture, which was nothing more than him reading aloud the captions of the pictures in the book while displaying slides of them on the screen at the front of the room. He followed that same mindless routine for two weeks, then gave us a test. The quiz consisted solely of him showing an apparently random selection of the same slides and asking us to write down the identifying information in the caption in the book—the same captions he had read aloud to us in lieu of holding a discussion, entertaining questions, or doing anything else remotely educational.

I aced the first test and soon figured out I didn't need to waste three hours each week sitting in a darkened classroom while this bozo read aloud from a book I could read myself. The schedule he'd distributed the first day had the test dates and pages in the text to be covered. All I had to do was memorize the captions the night before the test, show up that day, and collect my "A." I wasn't the only student who figured this out, so by the end of the semester, he was lecturing to an empty room. He got even by ignoring the test scores and failing anyone who had missed more than half his "lectures." This punished a good third of the class, including me. We protested to the dean and the instructor lost his job shortly thereafter, but the "F" stood. It dropped my GPA to 3.35, just a shade under the 3.5 required for cum laude status.

Other than that ugly incident, most of my college experiences were good. The college started a debate team and I not only tried out for it but got a scholarship as well. To earn it, I either competed on the debate team or appeared in theater productions, depending on my schedule at work. There wasn't a real auditorium when the campus first opened, but we were able to put on a production of a Carl Sandburg reader's theater program with a cast of five who sang, recited, and read his work in a large lecture hall. I played guitar and banjo as well as sang and acted. Later, once the fine arts building opened with a real theater, I played Hero, the male ingénue in "A Funny Thing Happened on the Way to the Forum."

The degree I earned in 1973 was a B.A. in Rhetoric and Public Address. I suspect it was the first and last degree in that field awarded by the school. It qualified me to get nothing like a real job but I found it perfect. The coursework included all sorts of communications theory, reading the classics from Socrates to Korzybski, and classwork on logic, ethics, and argumentation. Along the way, I also studied voice and articulation, which came in handy when I went to work in radio, as well as Old and Middle English, which enabled me to recite the Prologue to Chaucer's Canterbury Tales using the original tongue. That particular skill had no practical application but made for a fun party trick if enough alcohol was involved.

I also took a smattering of business courses with an eye to acquiring some knowledge that might be useful in earning a living. Accounting, marketing, and management courses balanced my study of rhetoric. I took economics, too, but made the mistake of enrolling in a night class. It was tough to stay awake for those three hour lectures on evenings when I started work at 6 AM each day.

The most life-altering thing I got out of college was a wife. I met Eileen in our freshman year in the campus mobile home that served as a student lounge. We dated, traveled together on the speech team, and got married during winter break the following January. We were 19 years old.

Eileen and I had a lot in common—maybe too much. She came from a difficult family situation similar to mine. She was also an intelligent woman and a good student, although she worked harder at her studies than I did. She was in college on a need scholarship funded by St. Patrick's Parish and worked part time as well. I often wonder how we ever found time to date given our school/work schedules, but we did.

I really got a kick out of her big Irish family. Every weekend, it seemed, they got together at somebody's house. There would be bottomless ice chests full of Budweiser and card games that went on for hours with dozens of little kids crawling around under the dining room table and cigarette smoke clouding the ceiling. I don't think I ever saw anyone get mad—we were all happy drunks, not fighting drunks.

Eileen's mother liked me and had no objection to our marriage. She only asked that we both finish college. She also suggested we get married in

January so guests could load up on gifts for us at white sales. She invited every human being she knew so we would get plenty of loot. The woman knew what she was doing. She also knew how much of that stuff we would need to set up a household.

We had a big Catholic wedding where my buddy, Dick, was best man and some of our friends from school provided the music. My gang gave me a bachelor party the night before that was just like the drunken bacchanals we'd had through high school. The guys chipped in to give me something I'd mentioned I wanted but couldn't afford—a plectrum banjo. I'm sure it was Dick's idea and I still have it.

We couldn't afford a honeymoon. In fact, the wedding was scheduled for Saturday so we wouldn't miss more than a day of work. We settled into a side-by-side duplex apartment that rented for $75 a month not including utilities. The old couple who owned it lived on the other side of the house and couldn't have been sweeter.

Eileen and I were happy—busy, but happy—struggling to make ends meet, working and going to school, and keeping house and socializing with friends and family. She had a slightly lighter work schedule than I did so she graduated on time in May, 1972. She also got pregnant on schedule, too, so that Jeremy would be born after I finished school the next winter. Eileen was an organized person.

Today, getting married at the age of 19 is considered ludicrous. At the time and place where we did it, though, it wasn't all that unusual. Most of the kids who married young weren't planning college, so a lot of them took the plunge right after high school. Even many of the college-bound kids tied the knot in their early twenties as soon as they had a degree and a job. We weren't outliers in that regard.

Neither of us admitted it at the time, but I've always felt we both saw marriage more as a way to get out of the home lives we had endured than anything else. Eileen had serious problems with her brother who lived at home that she always refused to talk about. I don't think there was anything untoward going on, but he was a heavy, heavy drinker who had suffered some sort of breakdown when their father abandoned them. Living with him in the house was hard on her. I was living my own bleak life in Lou's house and getting married gave me an excuse to leave.

On the positive side, though, I saw marriage as an adventure. I've always been game to try something different and setting up a new life with someone else certainly fit that bill. In a way, many other guys my age scratched that itch by going away to college or into the army. Not me—I got married.

1973

KFEQ Radio musicians, Bill Russell center with fiddle

Radio

My broadcasting career began with a small misunderstanding but it all worked out quite well in the end. It started during my freshman year in college as I was walking by the debate coach's office. He called out to ask me if I wanted a job. I thought he was looking for someone to carry some books to the library for him or something, so I stepped into his office. It turned out that a local radio station had called him to see if there were any students in a speech class who might be interested in working on the air. I thought about it for a few seconds, then answered, "No, thanks. I don't want to be a DJ." I was nothing if not a serious intellectual at the time. I wore a navy surplus pea coat and smoked a pipe and read Dostoyevsky very publicly.

"No," the coach said, "they need someone to do the news." That job appropriately enhanced my self-image, so I went for an audition.

At the radio station, the program director, Don "Cash" Register, sat me down in front of a microphone in a run-down recording studio and loaded a small reel of tape onto a machine. He handed me a few pages of copy torn from a teletype and told me to read it. After I ran through it the first time, he said, "Try it again, slower." I did and the audition was over. He took me and the tape in to see the station owner, Warren "Ward" Rhyner. Ward asked a few questions about my experience (none) and my work history (plenty), then asked me if I wanted a career in radio. I hadn't really thought about this as anything as grand as a career, but it had a nice ring to it.

"How much does it pay?" I asked.

"How much are you making now?" he answered.

"$2.35 an hour."

"That's fine," he said. "If you work out, you'll get a raise later."

It was clear I wasn't going to get rich in radio, but at least I wouldn't have to scrape grease from under my fingernails at the end of my shift. As a bonus, I had also received a valuable lesson in negotiation: when possible, name your own terms first—it's easier to talk down from your own than up from the other guy's.

Money aside, radio was great fun and it did turn out to be the foundation of my first real career. The station, KUSN AM/FM, was tiny and, I am sure, barely profitable. It simulcast its programming on both bands. The AM station was a 1,000-watt daytimer at 1270 on the dial, which meant its signal didn't cover much more than a couple of counties and it signed off when the sun went down. The FM station, 105.7, stayed on the air until midnight, but that didn't much matter since nobody owned FM receivers in those days—and they weren't widely available in cars until a few years later. None of these technical details mattered to me. I studied for and received a Third Class Radiotelephone Operator's license from the FCC—a process not quite as difficult as passing the written test for a driver's license—and I was ordained a broadcaster.

Between my job in radio and my classes at college, my schedule was a bit hectic but manageable. I stopped by the police station on my way to work about 5:30 every morning to check the blotter for newsworthy events that had occurred overnight, then went to the radio station by six AM to re-write local stories from the newspaper and clear the AP and UPI copy from the night before. My first deadline was for three headlines I had to read at 6:25 and my first newscast was at 6:55. My morning shift ended at nine, I dashed off to my first class of the day at 9:30, then came back for another shift from 1 to 5. Depending on my class schedule, I went back to school for night classes from 6:30 to 9:30 a couple of times a week. To fill out my 40-hour work week, I pulled a Saturday night shift as a DJ (lowering my standards in the service of income) and a Sunday morning sign-on stint playing pre-recorded religious programs.

The station had a jolly crew. Brother Bruce was the morning drive jock, so he was my companion at six AM sign-on. The shift didn't bother him since he was up at that hour anyway. Not sober, necessarily, but awake. He was a singer in a country band and typically closed whichever beer joint he was playing in at two AM or so, then unwound a bit with whatever woman-not-his-wife was handy. He usually stumbled in to the station just in time to sign on, often with a half pint of Seagram's Seven in his hip pocket to get him through the shift. One of my unofficial duties was to wake him up as the records ended so he could intro the next one before putting his head back down on the console.

The afternoon drive jock was Austin Lee. He was probably the most professional announcer on the staff and ran the tightest board in radio. In the analog days of live mics, turntables, and magnetic tape, it was a great point of pride to play your records, segue to commercials, deliver your patter, operate the control board, and otherwise perform your show single-handed (without an engineer) and without any dead air. Austin Lee was a master. He also had a smooth, deep, resonant delivery that belied his actual age—sixteen, just barely old enough to drive.

Then there was Tony, the self-proclaimed news director, who handled the news while I wasn't there and pulled weekend shifts as a jock using an air name I can't remember. He was a great guy but a bit of a radio nerd. He got his original job by volunteering to work for nothing on the weekends.

I made extra money—a big ten dollars—serving as the color man for the play-by-play announcer at high school football and basketball games. I didn't know, or care, much about the sports, but that that was okay since my real job was lugging around the Marti unit, a portable short-range remote transmitter that sent the commentary to the station for rebroadcast. During the game, I kept the stats for the play-by-play guy, who in real life was the station's ad sales manager. I wasn't very accurate with the stats and his play-by-play was not exactly gripping, but it didn't much matter; the games were on FM and no one could hear them anyway.

Much of what happened at KUSN and the characters involved could have been lifted whole from *WKRP in Cincinnati*, which aired on television not long after. Our receptionist was a knock-out blonde bombshell who could pass for Loni Anderson from the back. The sales manager wore obnoxious plaid sport coats just like Herb Tarleck. Tony, the self-appointed news director, may not have imitated a helicopter like Les Nessman, but he unscrewed the sign from the front of the Associated Press teletype machine and put it in the license plate holder on the front of his car so he could tool around town looking like a real reporter. And Dr. Johnny Fever? He was "Brother Bruce," of course, while "Cash" Register was Andy Travis, the professional but under-challenged program director.

Me? I was eighteen and having a blast. As the Saturday night jock, I could do what I wanted on the air as long as I stuck to the play list. One Fourth of July, I played fireworks sound effects while some of the other guys were up on the roof shooting Roman candles and bottle rockets over downtown St. Joseph. On Halloween, I adopted a cheesy Transylvanian accent and did my show as "Igor" until the station owner called and told me to cut it out.

The best part of Saturday night was when the groupies came around. Not that there were many of them, but enough. The station was on the top floor of the Howitt Building, a five-story office "tower" otherwise deserted on the weekends. It made for a great party scene as long as the main studio door was kept closed so no stray chatter and giggles could reach a live mic. The owner often monitored my show from home—probably the only listener it had. "Cash" Register, ostensibly my direct boss, was not a concern since he was likely to be one of the partiers, although he typically talked one of the girls into an audition and disappeared with her into his office early in the evening.

As the station's only real newsman, I covered city council meetings and mayoral press conferences when I wasn't in class. I made friends with the reporters from the other stations in town, and one of them, Dan Verbeck, told me his station had a new general manager and was looking for staff. KUSN was fun, but KFEQ was the big, established station in town so a job there would be a step up for me. Besides, I was married by then and needed the money. Rhyner had boosted my pay to $3.10 an hour, which still didn't cut the mustard when it came time to pay the rent, buy groceries, and buy schoolbooks. Fortunately, my tuition was covered by a debate team scholarship, which was similar to a football scholarship only our team didn't wear helmets or have cheerleaders.

The job I got at KFEQ encompassed everything from copy writing and commercial spot production to preparing the daily program logs. I also pulled weekend air shifts and subbed for Verbeck on the news from time to time. But it wasn't long before I needed more money despite the fact I was making about $5 an hour. I went to the station manager, a slimy accountant, who said I could make as much as I wanted by adding ad sales to my roster of duties. It didn't sound like something I wanted to do, and both Eileen and Mom advised against it, but the money could be good—if I actually sold anything.

It was a straight commission job, so there were no guarantees. The manager flipped open the Yellow Pages and wrote down twenty prospects for me. He told me to go to each one and offer them a package of a hundred spots for $300. For every sale I made, I would earn $36. The key, he told me, was to not give up on a prospect until they told me "no" three times.

My first sales call was on a roadside diner in Elwood, Kansas. The proprietor, a large woman wielding a spatula in a white waitress uniform, made me for a salesman as soon as I walked through the door. Somehow, I sensed she didn't want any radio advertising. In fact, I was pretty sure she didn't even want to talk about it. I knew this because as soon as I opened my mouth, she said flatly, "Get out."

"But," I said.

"Get out!" she repeated.

"But," I tried again.

She didn't say "Get out" again. Instead, she charged around the counter brandishing her spatula as if she were going to swat a fly—me. I took that as the third "no" and left in a hurry. Didn't leave her a coverage map or anything, just ran out the door and jumped into my car. It was a memorable start to what turned into a pretty successful sales career.

KFEQ was a radio station unlike anything you'll find on the air today. It signed on in 1923, which made it one of the country's pioneer commercial stations. One of the unique things I did there was to interview my grandfather as part of the station's fiftieth anniversary celebration in 1973. He had had a regular show on KFEQ in the 1930s in the days of live music. Even when I worked there, the station broadcast (and made most of its profit from) live farm news programs that aired twice daily. It still carried Kitchen Klatter, a syndicated talk show that was just what the name sounds like, and whatever music, from big bands to pop to semi-classical, the announcers felt like playing and talking about. When it finally switched to country music, the station dropped all the other garbage, but it kept the farm shows. They are still on the air today.

My schedule at KFEQ wasn't any less scrambled than it was at KUSN. I was at the station before and after class and actually did some station work preparing the program logs in school instead of listening to lectures in less-than-compelling classes. I worked weekends on the air and sold advertising whenever I had a spare couple of hours. During one Saturday air shift, I recorded an aircheck that happened to have a CBS News report about the return of Apollo 17 from the moon, which is how I know it was taped on December 16, 1972. My play list included Helen Reddy, Roger Whitaker, Peggy Lee, and Percy Faith (KFEQ wasn't exactly a progressive rock station) as well as commercials for some places only folks from St. Joseph would recognize: Leaverton Muffler, Bob Fay Appliances, Wolf's Camera, First Federal Savings & Loan, and Grocery Supply. I used the tape for auditions at big market stations, which is probably why my radio career ended in St. Joseph.

Not long after I started selling spots in my spare time, several members of the real sales staff departed for greener pastures. I jumped into one of their jobs and dropped my other duties. The timing couldn't have been better income-wise since Eileen was pregnant with Jeremy. She graduated that spring from MWSC while I finished up my degree that summer and the following fall semester. In the meantime, I had enough success in sales to attract the attention of the sales manager at KQTV, the local TV station, an ABC affiliate. He offered me a job that I jumped at. In January of 1974, just after I finished my college work, Jeremy was born. I told Eileen about my new job while she was in the hospital recovering. My radio career was over but TV was just beginning.

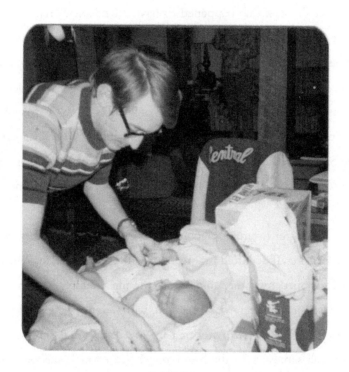

1974

1975

Birth

Congratulations! It's a boy.

Jeremy David

Joy!

Long, hard delivery for mom

Hours for me

No memory for you

Unless, yes, a dark wet passage

Into unbound love.

Crowded wait room, smoking.

Grandma and her sister with other fathers.

Finally I leave to breathe and smoke by myself

Until the news comes.

Mom damp browed but smiling

I grin in wonder,

Relief.

First day home on my lap

First book, *Treasure Island*

You quiet, listening to soft murmur of my voice

Feeding in my arms

First reading, Jim, Long John, Squire Trelawney

You quiet, nursing

Hearing the cadence

First nap against my chest

First bookmark, the mysterious map

You sleep, story-read and sated.

What sings in your sweet head?

Jeremy

Maybe I overdid the early teaching, but you seemed to like it and I couldn't see any harm, so you got a steady diet of word skills in a distinctly amateur but well-meant effort. As soon as you could hold your head steady in your baby carrier, I propped you up in front of the television screen when Sesame Street came on. By the time you could walk, Ernie was your favorite. When you started to make purposeful sounds, I made a set of hand-lettered flash cards with two-letter words on them. I would hold them up to you, say the words, and encourage you to repeat them. Within a few weeks, we graduated to three-letter words.

I read aloud to you every single day. Kids' books, sure, but also whatever I was reading at the time. You cuddled on my lap and then, when you got bigger, next to me in my chair. As I read, I traced a finger under the words to draw your eyes to them. I didn't slow down, just read aloud at a normal pace, figuring you would pick up the phonetics and grammar by osmosis or something. It must have worked, because by the time you could talk you could also read.

I don't know when, where, or how you learned arithmetic, although we did plenty of counting, adding, and subtracting with blocks and fingers and whatever else was handy in spare minutes here and there. Somehow, somewhere, you figured out the principles of division and asked me if you were right when you showed me how four fingers divided by two equals two fingers. You weren't four years old at the time.

In Chicago, you and I made frequent Saturday trips to the Field Museum of Natural History and the Museum of Science and Industry. Your preference was a toss-up. The Museum of Science and Industry had more hands-on kid-friendly things to do, but the Field Museum had dinosaurs. I think the monster bones won, but it's hard to say.

You were kindergarten age when we moved to New Rochelle, but starting school at that level would have been wrong for you. We'd already gone through the testing process in Chicago so you could skip kindergarten and the school in New Rochelle agreed to start you in first grade when they saw that you were already reading at a sixth-grade level.

Does *Treasure Island* live somewhere in your subconscious? Are you twin to Jim Hawkins, that bright, resourceful lad who overcame his fatherless state to beat Long John Silver and the pirate gang? I hope so.

Leigh Anna

Leigh Anna

"**Y**our wife is fine, Mr. Donelson," the doctor says, "although we have her sedated right now."

I stand exhausted in the institutionally-tiled hallway outside the delivery room. They brought me here instead of to the fathers' waiting room for some reason—maybe because it is more convenient for the doctor, who probably wants to just slip away quickly after he speaks to me. It isn't a good spot, though, because there is no place for me to sit down while he gives me the rest of his news. When he delivers it, I slump against the pale green wall.

"The baby is a girl but she has Down syndrome," he says. I must look as blank as I feel because he adds, "That means she is mongoloid."

He catches me before I can slide down the wall. Bright motes flicker in my eyes. A rushing roar fills my ears. I don't breathe. His touch brings me out of a faint before I fall.

"Are you okay, Mr. Donelson?"

I nod and swallow. I am not okay. I realize I am not breathing, so I make myself suck air in, let it out. In and out.

.

"Your wife doesn't know. I wanted to talk to you first. It would be best for everyone if the baby goes into an institution right away before Eileen becomes too attached to it. Do you want us to take care of that?"

I don't understand. It's coming too forcefully, too fast to comprehend. What is he saying?

The doctor looks over his shoulder at the door to the delivery room. Then he turns to me and stiffens his back. His speech becomes clipped, officious. "Let me be blunt. A child like this will not develop normally. It will be retarded and have health problems. It will disrupt your lives. It might even destroy them. The best place for it is the state hospital where professionals can look after it."

I blurt, "But it's a baby—our baby." I vaguely realize what he's pushing me to do but I can't bring myself to agree. How could I do that? Besides, shouldn't Eileen have a say?

"It won't live a normal life and neither will you," he says. "I've seen marriages fall apart over things like this. You're both young and healthy. You have a son already and you can have more." He must see alarm in my eyes when he mentions Jeremy. "Besides, it won't be fair to your little boy to grow up with a sister like this."

He's pressuring me. Why is he pushing so hard? I don't like to be told what to do, so I press back with what little strength I can muster.

"Let me see Eileen," I say. "I want to talk to her."

"Of course," he says. "She won't be thinking clearly, but I will explain the options and you can both decide."

The doctor is right; Eileen is not thinking clearly. Neither am I. The enormity of the decision he is pressing on us crushes rational thought and leaves space for only one of two responses, a puny "yes" or a screaming "NO." When the doctor asks if he can start the placement process, Eileen shakes her head. He raises an eyebrow and looks at me but I just glare back

192

at him. I hold her hand while she nods off. The doctor starts to say something more, then drops his head and leaves the room without further comment.

After I am sure Eileen is asleep, I leave the recovery room to find the nursery. I knock on the window and ask the nurse if I can see our baby. She smiles and points to a little bundle lying motionless in a crib on the other side of the viewing window. All I can see between the swaddling wrap and her tiny skull cap is her smooth face, eyes closed and shaped oddly in a way I can't quite identify, nose scrunched up, her tongue peeking from between her lips. She looks healthy to me, but she is still, very, very still. If she moved a bit, waved an arm in the air or just turned her head, my heart would twist with an aching love. But she doesn't move and her stillness is unnatural. It leaves me wondering about my own lack of feeling. I must be tired, I think. Emotionally drained.

I leave the hospital and drive directly to the library a few blocks away. The card catalog shows a scant half dozen books with references to Down Syndrome and mongolism, none published within my lifetime. I settle into a table in the reference room and read everything available. I learn nothing good. When the books were written, few people with Down Syndrome lived past forty. Nearly all were institutionalized from birth and never learned even rudimentary life skills, much less how to read and write. The doctor's recommendation was very much in line with the practices of pre-WWII medicine. There was one vague reference to studies being done to determine the effects of stimulation and more progressive care, but at the time it was written, nothing had been determined. I don't know what, if anything, I will tell Eileen about my research.

I also am not sure what to tell our family and friends about the birth. They know Eileen went into the hospital, but she had asked everyone to stay away, telling them I would let them know when the baby arrives. I will make those calls when I get home, but not until I know what to say. Anyone calling the hospital, I assume, will be told mom and baby are doing fine. There are no cell phones, so it is easier to control your privacy.

Back at the hospital, I find Eileen sitting up in bed with the baby in her arms. A nurse passes me with a side-long glance as I come in. I sit down on the edge of the bed. The baby's eyes are open, but like all babies, it is clear she can't see. She makes nursing motions with her mouth, her tiny tongue going in and out. One hand, free of the blanket, waves feebly in the air. I put a finger into her palm, but she doesn't grip it.

Eileen lifts her gaze from the baby and looks at me, her eyes defiant. "Her name is Leigh Anna—named after your mom and mine," she says. "They are not going to take this baby away from me."

"Okay," I answer. The decision had been made. Many, many others— family, friends, professionals—will try to change our minds in the next few days. They will talk to us formally and directly or drop hints and send not-so-subtle signals; they will warn us of grief and heartbreak to come. But it doesn't matter. Eileen never questions our decision and neither do I. Leigh Anna has a place in our now-uncertain future.

1983

1980

Ghost

I used to delight in the shivers raised by a well-wrought ghost story and got perverse pleasure out of movies where things go bump in the night. It was all fun, even though I never believed in supernatural beings, spooks, or spectres. I changed my mind about such things, though, when a ghost tried to kill my children.

Even now, after all that happened, I'm still not entirely convinced that ghosts exist, although I don't believe they don't, either. There are perfectly rational explanations for all the events my kids and I lived through, but I can no longer accept them without question no matter how scientific they are. What I do have now is a healthy respect for the possibility that spirits exist. In fact, that respect led me to do things a completely rational person would never do. Things I felt I had to do to keep my family alive.

Many ghost stories begin when the innocent victims-to-be move into an old house. That's when our story starts as well, when we settled into our new home in New Rochelle in 1979. It was a non-descript three-story frame house with a dark, brick-walled basement and a finished attic, one of three once-identical houses built side by side in a quiet neighborhood near Iona College in 1920. There were four small bedrooms and a cramped bath on the second floor and a kitchen, living room, and dining room on the first. It was perfect for us since Jeremy and Leigh Anna could each have their own rooms and Eileen could use the extra bedroom as a sewing room unless we had guests, which would be infrequent given that our families were half a continent away and not financially capable of much travel.

It was an old house but it had good bones. It was solid even though the floors creaked a bit and the stairs a bit more, but that was to be expected. Most of the double-hung windows worked pretty well and even those where the sash weights had come loose were easy to repair. They all rattled a bit in the wind, but again, that is to be expected in an old house. The plumbing worked, the boiler was ancient but sound, and the radiators hissed and bubbled just enough to show they were in working order.

The attic had possibilities, although we weren't sure for what. It was reached by a narrow staircase that was behind a door in the second floor hall almost opposite the stairway that led down to the first floor. When I first saw it, the thought occurred to me that if someone tripped at the top of the attic stairs, they could tumble all the way to the foyer on the first floor. As you climbed the stairs, your back was to the rest of the attic and every time I went up them, I felt compelled to look up over my shoulder to see if there were eyes watching me. Once you reached the top of the stairs and turned around, you were in a center hall with two rooms on either side. Each room had knee walls and nooks of their own that provided numerous places for hiding just around a corner.

Someone had once lived in the attic, although not recently. The walls were decorated with murals, amateurish scenes painted directly on the plaster. The colors were faded, the paint cracked and peeling in places. The artist had painted verdant forests and fields of yellow grain, a farm house or two, some dirt roads, all from the viewpoint of someone far away and on high as if standing on a mountain top. Oddly, there weren't any people depicted in any of the panels. I deduced they were painted sometime in the 1930s from the biplane cruising through the sky in one of them. That would also explain the condition of the paint. Later, after things started happening up there, it occurred to me as strange that during nearly fifty years, none of the previous owners had touched those walls or their lifeless, fading murals.

I went up alone to inspect it on the day of our closing. The realtor was too fat to make the climb and Eileen didn't need to. The rooms were empty and, unlike the rest of the house, they hadn't been swept after the old owners moved out. The heavy dust on the floor, in fact, looked like it hadn't been disturbed in years except for the footprints I left when we first looked at the house before we decided to buy it. The windows were grimy and turned the bright sunshine from outside into a pale, diffuse glow in the rooms.

Alone in the silent space during the walk-through, I felt there was something lurking in every nook or behind every doorway, something waiting to grab me. The rooms were small and I always seemed to be just a step or two from a blind corner. I found myself listening hard to detect another presence, but heard nothing but my own shallow breathing in the oppressive silence. Just then, the realtor shouted up the stairs that we had to go. My heart jumped into my throat and I choked off a scream.

The attic faded into the back of my mind once we moved in and started dealing with the other idiosyncrasies of the house. It was an old place with wood floors that creaked and doors that rattled in the wind. The first night in our new bedroom, the random groans and odd pops of the place kept me awake for a while. I finally dropped off, only to be startled full awake by the sharp squeal of a hinge. When my heart stopped racing, I realized the closet door next to my side of the bed stood open. I knew it had been closed when I went to bed. I tensed to jump up, then lay back as I reminded myself that the house was far from square or level, having settled unevenly into its foundation over the past half century. When Eileen loaded the closet rods and shelves, I thought, the weight must have altered the door frame's geometry enough to loosen the catch. I got up, closed the door, and mentally added it to my long list of repairs. By the next day I had forgotten all about it.

~~§~~

When it happened again the next night, though, I sat straight up in bed sure that someone or some thing was coming through the closet door after me. I calmed down when I realized where I was, though, and glanced at the alarm clock. It was 3:15 AM.

As the days and nights passed, the door seemed to swing open every night at the same time--or so I imagined. I often wonder if I simply projected the time onto the actual experience as a result of reading *The Amityville Horror* shortly before we moved. The protagonist, George DeFeo, awoke each morning at 3:15 in his haunted house, too. That was the hour the previous owner had murdered his family in their sleep. My over-active brain may have imagined the time, but the closet door opened every night until I finally put a hook and eye latch on it to keep it closed.

A few days later, I put identical latches on all the doors upstairs. Leigh Anna was toddling around and could work a doorknob perfectly well. I decided the easiest way to baby proof the bedrooms was simply to keep her out of them. I put the latches out of her reach but within Jeremy's. Even then, I kept finding the hook on the door to the attic staircase undone, but wrote it off to someone bumping the door in passing. I didn't connect it to everything else until later.

Doors that unlocked and opened themselves weren't the house's only mystery. One of the first projects I undertook was to brighten up our bedroom with wallpaper. I'd done plenty of papering and this didn't present any special challenges aside from having to fit everything around the windows, none of which were perfectly square. I got it done in a day, and cleaned up the room so we could sleep there the same night. Just after Eileen and I climbed into bed, though, I heard a peculiar gentle scratching. I turned on a light only to find a long curl of wallpaper lying on the floor across the room. While I watched, another strip peeled down the wall. Strip after strip loosed itself as it someone had slipped a fingernail under the top edge and pulled it free. The strangest part of it was that each one came off individually in turn as if waiting for the one before it to be finished. The next day, I gathered up all the expensive wallpaper and threw it away, then prepped and painted the walls. At the time, I just assumed I had made a mistake with the adhesive or something. Given what happened later, I'm not so sure.

A few weeks after we moved in, I got around to taking on the attic project. We thought it would make a perfect play room for Jeremy, who was filling his bedroom with Star Wars paraphernalia and other stuff, and later for Leigh Anna, whose doll collection was getting out of hand. I spent a Saturday morning in the attic washing the windows and running the vacuum cleaner over the ceilings and walls as well as the floors. I opened all the crawlspaces in the knee walls, too, and attacked the decades of dust in them with a vengeance. The morning outside was bright, making it easier for me to suppress the feeling that my every move was being watched.

Just before I quit for lunch, I noticed a trap door to the peak of the roof above the attic ceiling. I stood on a chair and shoved it open so I could get my head inside. At first, I didn't see anything except dust motes, but as my eyes adjusted to the gloom they caught a glint of light on something wedged between the rafters. It was an empty half-pint bottle that had once held

Chicken Cock whiskey, a brand I've since learned was a mainstay of bootleggers who smuggled it in from Canada. Next to it was an empty pay envelope from the Roosevelt Hotel in New York City. It wasn't dated, but the wages were minuscule. Just as I had thought, someone—a boarder perhaps—had at one time lived in this attic. Could it have been the artist? Impossible to tell, but the time frame seemed consistent. Somehow the relics humanized the spirit that I felt watching me the entire time I was there. I started to throw my finds into the trash, but then changed my mind and put the treasures back where I found them. For some reason, I felt relieved by my decision.

I went back to the attic after lunch to finish prepping the walls and ceiling for painting. I kind of hated to obliterate the murals, but they were dismal and certainly not something you'd find on the walls of a playroom. My intention was to wash all the surfaces thoroughly, let them dry a week, then paint the following weekend.

The afternoon sun glared through the newly-clean windows and deepened the shadows in the rest of the attic. I hauled a bucket of sudsy water up the stairs and covered the floor of the room in the front side of the house so I could wash the ceiling and walls. I used a sponge mop to reach the ceiling and worked slowly, trying to keep the drips and runoff to a minimum, but the cleaning solution still seeped down across the murals in dirty streaks. As the sun sank lower in the sky, the shadows in the room darkened along with my enthusiasm for the project. Odd reflections caught in my glasses every time I lifted the mop. When I turned around to see what caused them, the shadows moved, too. Just a hair, but as if they were contracting back to normal size from a slight bulge in my direction. Must be ammonia fumes from the detergent playing tricks with my head, I thought. By the time I finished the ceiling in the first room, I realized it was going to take much longer than I planned to get rid of the grime on the murals. No way could I finish today. I briefly considered setting up some work lights, but I didn't want to be up there after dark.

Eileen took Jeremy to church the next morning. I was happy to stay home with Leigh Anna and delayed working in the attic until that afternoon. Leigh Anna played with her dolls while I read the newspaper and enjoyed a laid-back Sunday morning. Before she left, Eileen reminded me to take Leigh Anna to the toilet on the hour every hour whether she wanted to go or not. She was potty training at the time so consistency was essential. Dutifully, I took her upstairs at eleven and praised her profusely when she tinkled in the toilet. The bathroom was tiny, just large enough for the essentials with barely enough room between the tub and sink for me to kneel and pull up Leigh Anna's pants. As I finished and leaned back on my heels to stand up, the heavy glass globe on the ceiling light fixture fell and crashed to the floor right between us. It missed our heads by inches. Leigh Anna screamed as I snatched her up. I backed quickly out of the room and slammed the bathroom door behind us. Amazingly, neither one of us had been struck by flying glass. If the heavy globe had hit either of us on the head, the blow would have been brutal if not fatal.

Once I got Leigh Anna calmed down and playing with her dolls in her bedroom, I went back to the bathroom to sweep up the glass. I examined the remains of the fixture carefully. Three set screws held the eight-inch frosted glass globe in a metal bracket on the ceiling and all the parts seemed perfectly fine. I'd never had reason to inspect it before, so I suppose it's possible the globe had been loose since before we moved in. Maybe I bumped the wall and shifted the globe off its bracket without realizing it. Maybe. There was no other rational explanation as to why it chose that moment to drop, however. No rational reason at all.

Instead of going back to work in the attic that Sunday afternoon, I went to buy a globe to replace the one that shattered. By the time I finished, it was too late in the day to start again on the attic project. I was relieved.

~~§~~

A week passed. We stayed busy as usual, work, school, play, breakfast, lunch, dinner, bedtime. I was busy enough to push thoughts of the close call out of my mind and drank enough vodka each evening to fall immediately to sleep. It was not a restful sleep, though, and the next Saturday morning I awakened with a start at 3:15. The closet door had tried to open and was settled against the hook and eye. I lay awake until nearly dawn listening to the pops and creaks of the old house.

When I went back to the attic that morning, it was creepier than ever. I heard quiet rustlings behind every wall and the sunlight steaming through the windows had a harshness to it that cast black shadows into every corner. As I puttered about half-heartedly moving drop cloths from place to place, I sensed more strongly than ever that I was not just being watched but that someone was sneaking up on me from behind. I whirled around once, twice, then a third time but nothing was there. Get a grip on it, I told myself. I picked up the sponge mop I had been using to wash the walls and realized I had left the buckets of water and cleaning solution in the kitchen. Reprieved, I went downstairs to get them.

Eileen had taken Leigh Anna shopping that morning and Jeremy was playing quietly in his room. I left the attic door open since I would have both hands full when I came back up.

The buckets were where I had left them but I was in no hurry to return upstairs. I poured a cup of cold, leftover coffee and put it in the microwave. Just as it dinged completion I heard Jeremy running down the stairs.

"Dad!" he called.

"In the kitchen," I answered.

He came through the doorway with wild eyes, his face pale.

"What's wrong?" I demanded.

"Somebody," he said, breathless, his voice barely above a whisper. "tried to shove me down the stairs."

"What do you mean?" I knelt so I could look directly into his face.

"I was standing at the top of the stairs," he answered, "And I felt somebody push my back."

I tried to keep panic off my face as I put a hand on his shoulder. "Are you okay?"

"Yeah. I grabbed the banister and it quit pushing."

My entire body went cold. "You're sure you're okay?" I repeated.

"Yeah. I'm okay," he answered. "What was it?"

I searched my blank brain for a plausible answer. "The wind . . . I mean, a draft. From the attic. I was working up there and you probably felt a puff of air coming down the stairs." It was lame, but all I could summon at the moment. "Okay?"

Jeremy's face was full of doubt, but at least the fear was gone from his eyes. "I guess so."

"Don't run on the stairs again," I said to further distract him. "You know better than that. Your mother would kill you if she found out." Maybe, just maybe, he would think twice before mentioning the scare to Eileen.

"Can I go outside?" he asked, squirming out of my grip and heading for the back door.

"Sure, just stay in the yard," I called after him.

My knees quivered as I stood up, my body cold as if no blood were circulating. With Jeremy out of the room, I succumbed to the fright and leaned against the kitchen counter. This was too much for my rational mind to accept. I could sort of explain everything else—the closet door that opened on its own, the spooky feeling I got working alone in the shadow-filled attic, even the light fixture that fell as Leigh Anna and I stood beneath it—but I could not explain this. Jeremy was too smart, too level-headed, too mature to mistake a puff of wind for what he felt. He also had no reason to make anything like this up. I'd been careful to keep all the oddities I found about the house to myself. I'd not mentioned any of it to Eileen and certainly never said anything to Jeremy. This really happened and I really couldn't explain it.

I heard Jeremy climbing on the swing set in the back yard but looked out to check on him just the same. He's fine, I thought. At least for now.

But something had to be done. My mind leaped to the obvious solution. We would sell the house and move! But how would I explain that to Eileen? She wasn't happy in New York as it was and hearing a ghost story from me wasn't going to make her any happier. Besides, we had sunk everything we had—as well as a sizable loan from the company I worked for—into the house less than a year ago. How could we finance another purchase and move? Something told me a quick re-sale would end up costing us money we simply didn't have. We were stuck in the house. And living with an increasingly angry spirit.

At a loss, I decided to try to pacify the ghost or whatever it was. Now was the time to do it, too, while Jeremy was outside, before Eileen came home, and while I was desperate and charged by adrenaline.

I forced myself up the stairs to the second floor. The attic door was closed. I was sure I had left it open. It made me even more determined to do what I had to do. I yanked open the narrow door and stomped up the stairs.

I may have been scared witless inside, but I knew I had to make a show of strength.

I turned at the top of the stairs and took three resolute steps to the center of the attic where the rooms opened off the hallway. I stood in the hall between them and used my deepest, most powerful voice.

"All right. You win," I said. I waited, but was answered by silence as if the attic were holding its breath. "Here's the deal. You can have the attic but we need the rest of the house. I won't bother you up here and you don't bother us down there. I may store some stuff here, but that's just for appearances. No playroom. No more clean up. Nothing but a few boxes. The attic is all yours and you will not be bothered again. You just have to leave us alone downstairs. That's the deal. As of today. Agreed?"

Silence. I stood perfectly still waiting for a sign but got nothing. I counted silently to ten, turned around once in a complete circle to see if there was anything behind me, then headed back to the stairs. As I turned my back on the attic, for the first time I felt alone. No one was watching. No one was creeping up on me from behind. I descended the stairs slowly, closed the door after myself, and slid the hook into the eye.

I upheld our end of the bargain by telling Eileen the attic was too drafty to be a playroom. I replaced the hook and eye with a sturdy barrel bolt. Aside from a few boxes of Christmas ornaments, we didn't store much up there. Years later, after Eileen had moved out with the kids and I lived there alone, I still never stepped foot in the attic.

1977

Spanking

Dear Jeremy,

I spanked you once, and for that among many other things I hope you will forgive me.

Your initial transgression is lost to me now but I know why I delivered the spanking. I also know why my seemingly trivial action—spanking isn't exactly unheard of in our society—stayed with me all these years. The reason I remember it lies in the very fact that the provocation has faded while the shame of what I did burns brightly.

You may remember the spanking, although I hope not. You were six years old and your crime was completely banal. I found out what you did, scolded you for it, then calmly, without rage or anger, pulled you over my knee and smacked your behind with my open hand until you cried. I hit you three times. Then I stood you up, made you promise to never do whatever it was you had done again, and sent you sobbing to your room. I am sure your tears came not from the pain I inflicted but from the humiliation of it all. Perhaps also from the shocking revelation that the father who loved you without reservation was also willing to hurt you.

I could blame the whole thing on the way I was treated by my stepfathers, but that would not be entirely accurate. Walt spanked me, that's for sure, but not often and not brutally. Lou's abuse was more frequently verbal; I was too old for spanking by the time he came into my life and, besides, I was so scared of him when I was twelve that I never gave him cause. Both men threatened to "get the belt" from time to time, but I seldom recall them following through on that threat with me, although they did frequently with my brothers.

It sounds ugly, but I spanked you to prove I could, to impress on you, and more importantly, on myself, that I had the power to do it. It was a conscious expression of my physical supremacy over the other people in my cave, an arrogant alpha act of dominance, each blow on your defenseless butt a notch in the handle of my manliness. You were just a pawn, your crime simply an excuse. Like many innocent victims, you were in the wrong place at the wrong time and I took advantage of it. I wasn't teaching you a lesson, I was indulging my id.

And for a minute or so it felt good. While you promised between sobs to never do it again, I struggled to keep from smirking. It was at that moment, the instant when I realized I enjoyed the triumph of physically dominating a child a third my size, that I saw I wasn't all-powerful—I was just an asshole. I felt myself becoming my stepfathers, smug and swaggering, and I didn't like myself at all.

The next thought I had was of you. What was that look I saw in your eyes? Fear? Shame? Resentment? Reproach? Disappointment? I suspect your true feelings swirled in the chaos of the moment like mine, flying from coherent anger to non-verbal moans of raw terror.

Or maybe you had expected it all along, were reconciled to the prospect that your father, a bully, was going to take the next step and beat you someday. I hope not, but now that I'd performed such a revealing act, how could I know your thoughts?

Three blows. No paddle or hairbrush or belt. No bare buttocks. Not even much power behind the blows. But harmful just the same. Maybe to you, certainly to me.

Jeremy

Divorce

The divorce came on suddenly. Like coming down with pneumonia, I went to bed feeling fine, then woke up the next day miserable and bewildered. And just like from pneumonia, my chest ached and I couldn't take a deep breath without sharp pain that lasted for weeks, leaving me with weakness that lingered for years.

While it came as a surprise to me, Eileen had planned it for at least a year. I never forgave her for that. On the other hand, if I hadn't been so oblivious, I would have known something was seriously wrong. Her headaches became more frequent a couple of years before she told me she wanted a divorce and our physical relationship had dwindled to nothing. She began hanging out with her co-workers after work, something I thought was perfectly innocent at the time since I did plenty of socializing of my own with clients in the evenings. Before that began, though, she started paying stricter than usual attention to our household finances, which she had always managed in her very capable manner. She told me when the settlement discussions began that she had succeeded in paying off all our debts except our mortgage during the preceding year so she could make a clean break. I admired her for doing that while I shuddered at its cold-bloodedness.

We took a brief vacation without the kids to "rekindle the fires," but that warmth lasted about as long as the sunburn she got on the beach in Puerto Rico. We visited a marriage counselor a few times, but I gave it up when she couldn't—or wouldn't—give any specific reason for wanting out of our marriage other than the big one: she just didn't love me anymore. And no, there wasn't anything I could do, no change I could make, no course of treatment that would heal us. She didn't want to talk about it, so we didn't.

Not a pretty picture, is it? As divorces go, though, this one was mostly devoid of drama. It was very efficient.

For years, I've wondered why Eileen decided she didn't want to be married to me. I can think of several possible reasons and, like most such decisions, it was probably based on a combination of all of them. Alcohol may have played a role, although at that point it didn't yet control my life. I also was not a mean or abusive drunk. If anything, booze made me loving and sentimental. I wanted to cuddle, not fight. Of course, a sloppy, smelly drunk isn't very appealing to anyone except another sloppy, smelly drunk, so I can't use that as a defense. Still, I can't recall a time when my drinking affected the kids or Eileen.

It could have been the amount of time and energy I devoted to work, but I don't think I did more of that than is normal for any ambitious up-and-comer. Yes, there were evenings when I had to entertain clients and often came home soused, but those weren't daily events and I never stopped off for a quick one with the boys (or girls) after work unless there were clients involved. Instead, I religiously caught the 5:28 every night, which brought me through the front door before 6:30—an accomplishment not many commuters with jobs like mine can claim. We ate a family dinner that I cooked while Eileen was getting the kids ready for bed almost every night and weekends were for the family—chores around the house, Little League, shopping, museums, things we did together. We may not have lived an Ozzie and Harriet life, but we tried. It was enough for me, but Eileen found it lacking.

Eileen told me she wanted a divorce one night after we had finished dinner and tucked the kids into bed. The news came as a double shock since I had spent the entire day in a golden glow mentally celebrating the successes of my life. Just that week I had bought my first Brooks Brothers suit, a reward I had promised myself when my annual earnings hit $100,000—a lot of money to me at the time. Jeremy was playing baseball and I was coaching the team. I had gone for lunch that day to "Jazz at Noon" where I relaxed and enjoyed the music before going back to the office for a rare stress-free afternoon and an early train home. Oddly, I don't recall her exact words that night, but I remember how I spent the day. Oblivious? Yes, without a doubt.

It may have been my detachment that grated on Eileen the same way it probably bothers others close to me. I often live in my own head, not sharing my thoughts with anybody because I usually don't think to. I've also never felt compelled to prattle on just to fill a conversational void, and I suppose that can be taken as aloofness or disengagement or lack of interest in the other person—in this case, Eileen. I believe though, that one true test of how close you are to someone is how long you can be comfortable with them without speaking. Most people can't stand silence. They make small talk, turn on the radio or television, babble on the phone or do all at once in a cacophonous effort to keep from exercising their brains. I am just the opposite. Silence is my milieu. I don't talk unless I have something to say. I don't play music just to have some noise in the background. Some would say I live in a shell of my own making and they would be correct.

That's not to say I can't have a conversation; I like chatting with people about the events of the moment, debating opinions, listening to their thoughts. In fact, I am a very good listener for the simple reason I'm fully engaged in the process and not compelled to hear the sound of my own voice.

Most people aren't listening when someone else is talking; instead, they are concentrating on what their own response will be. Since I am not worried about responding, I can invest my energy in actually hearing the other person. That was one of my strengths, I always thought, and my success in sales and management proves the point.

It works to strengthen personal relationships, too. I would always listen to Eileen, ask her opinion, weigh (or more likely defer to) her views on major decisions like buying a house or a car. But our conversations were generally purposeful and businesslike. She said once during a marriage therapy session that we made a good team, we were good partners, but that it wasn't enough. She was right. We needed a little romance—maybe a lot of romance—and I've never been able to express those feelings in a natural, easy manner. I made a point of saying "I love you" every day, but it was just another task on my to-do list. I offered sincere praise, but probably not often enough. I believe compliments for the sake of form are shallow and denigrate the worth of full, honest praise. Maybe I'm wrong in that, but I won't be changing anytime soon.

There were some who thought Leigh Anna's handicap drove us apart, but they were dead wrong. If anything, Leigh Anna's birth brought us closer together, united in an effort to do the best for her and to stand firm against those who said she should be institutionalized. Oh yes, it wasn't just the doctor who recommended it. One of Eileen's cousins said so, too, and I'm sure many others thought the same thing but expressed it only through their pitying eyes. Eileen was very sensitive to them and her jaw would tighten when she talked about what various ones had said or telegraphed with their body language when they held the baby. She had a fierce temper but, much like me, she held it in, drawing strength from it and allowing it to corrode her relationships. Perhaps we both would have been better off expressing anger more freely.

As Leigh Anna grew, our campaign to overcome her handicap took up a fair amount of time and energy, but we approached it as a team. We saw the doctors and therapists together, took turns stimulating her and doing her exercises, feeding, bathing, and changing her diapers—much the same way we took care of Jeremy when he was a baby only with more intensity of purpose, if that is possible. In Chicago and later in New York, we joined parent support groups that further united us in our cause. There is no question that Leigh Anna's birth put stress into our lives, but it didn't destroy our marriage.

If I were forced to point to something that did, however, I would say that my decisions—and they were mine, not hers—to move from little old St. Joseph to great big Chicago and then to other-wordly New York sealed our fate. Leigh Anna was just six months old when I started my new job in Chicago. Eileen stayed behind to sell the house while I lived with her brother, Dan, in South Park. We'd talked the decision through, but deep in her heart Eileen didn't want to leave. It was an important if not essential career move for me and opened up a world of resources for Leigh Anna and Jeremy that we would never find in St. Joseph, but the move took Eileen out of the tribal cocoon that enveloped her. If her brother hadn't already taken that step, I don't think she would have agreed.

Our life in Chicago was stressful, at least for her. I was riding a rocket to the stars, learning a whole new business, socializing with a big-city crowd at work, and proving myself very good at it. Eileen, though, had left a brand new three-bedroom home that was the envy of her friends and was stuck in an apartment half its size with two pre-school kids. She couldn't get a job until the kids were in school and that crushed her spirit. She had been a proud working woman in St. Joseph; now she was a *haus frau* with a husband enjoying what looked like a glittering professional life. That hurt.

217

Just as the wound began to heal—we made a down payment on a house in Chicago and she started looking for day care for the kids and a job for herself—we moved to New York. Again, it was an essential career move for me, a nasty gut-punch for her. Jeremy was ready to start school and Leigh Anna had just learned to walk. Amid all that, we had to find a home, move, and start all over finding the resources and support we needed. The big city scared Eileen, too, mostly because it was even farther from her family. We could drive between Chicago and St. Joseph, but New York was too far away.

She was never happy there. Once the kids got in school and daycare, she found a job that helped but didn't cure her unhappiness. Her commute was tough—Metro North then the subway—until she transferred to an office in Stamford. My job responsibilities kept expanding so I traveled more, entertained more, and was even more often mentally absent. We had nice neighbors and both of us had friends at work, but none close enough to replace her family. Add in the stresses of finding the right school environment for Leigh Anna, after-school care for both kids, and the normal strains of two people in their twenties trying to get ahead in the world, then take away the family support she needed, and a divorce happened.

To this day, I have only unconfirmed suspicions of what went wrong. I tend to place the blame on me, not Eileen, although looking back now through the long, obscuring fog of time, I don't accept all of it. In fact, I've come to believe there's no reason to blame anybody for anything. We didn't commit a crime—we got a very civil divorce to end a marriage that was probably doomed from the start. We were virtually children when we got married. It's a wonder it lasted as long as it did. We got a lot of things right, too, especially raising two wonderful kids. We did that both together and individually and took joy in it. The birthday parties, teaching Jeremy to read and ride a bike, Little League, even Leigh Anna's therapies and exercises, were deeply satisfying to us both. The divorce itself we managed as well as we could to make it easy on the kids. We had both seen it happen otherwise and were not going to expose Jeremy and Leigh Anna to the ugliness we had gone through. So where's the crime? Why should I feel guilty?

Divorce is not scarlet-letter-worthy these days, but it often causes a passing look askance even by those who have experienced it themselves. The divorced are damaged goods, relationship impaired, failures in one of life's major tasks. Which is stupid, of course. They used to be married and then they chose not to be. I used to play tennis but then I decided not to. I used to drive a Chevy, now I own a Toyota. What's the difference? Especially what's the difference to you, idle bystander? I don't need your pity and I don't deserve your judgment.

So who was to blame? Me, I guess, both directly and indirectly. My basic crime was ambition, the desire to prove my ability to escape the world I grew up in. Compounding it was my introspective personality and growing attraction to alcohol. Of course, it may also be that I'm simply not suited for marriage at all.

Ultimately, Eileen wanted one life and I wanted another. Neither of us was wrong, but we sure could have talked about it more. I don't know if we could have reconciled our individual desires, but there would have been a chance to. At the least, I would have been aware of her feelings before they became hardened into stone. If I had understood them, I could possibly have adapted to or changed her attitude, but we'll never know.

Looking back after her passing, I forgive Eileen for what she did to me and the kids. I wonder if she forgave me.

The Talk

Telling your son you must leave him

Is to step off the edge of the earth into the

    Void.

Empty, black, numb,

You leave him with fallen fumbling words,

Leaves sere and crumbling.

Not your fault

I am sure you never thought so until we planted the idea.

Grownup's love may wither but never mine for you

Always be your dad

Always be there

Unless, until, I'm not.

My thought but not spoken,

You don't know, but I do.

My own dad was gone before I knew him.

He was there like Halley's Comet

Remembered more for his absence.

This threatens us, but I won't say it.

For me,

    Void.

I cried twice in my adult life

Once, when I told my son.

Decades later when I told my therapist

About telling my son.

Each pierced the callus over my heart,

The only dagger sharp enough.

We are today tougher.

Void still lies beneath me.

1959

Baseball

I stand in the coach's box at first base focused on Jeremy as he steps up to bat. He is a veteran now—seven years in Little League, level-headed, relaxed at the plate. He takes a practice swing, then another, then settles into the batters' box, his eyes on the pitcher, his left foot back next to the right with the heel lifted so most of his weight is on his right leg and he's ready to step into the pitch. That's what I taught him and seeing it brings me back to my time in the batter's box.

I am eight years old and afraid at the plate. I don't fear failure; I am simply scared of the ball. It is hard and I am soft. The pitcher eyeing me is ten, which makes him two years older than I am, and taller by at least a head. I know he throws hard. He knows I am afraid. I push the heavy batting helmet off my forehead and look down the first base line to Walt in the coach's box.

My stepdad is the reason I am here. I like baseball well enough, but I'm not much of a ball player. He thinks, though, that playing the game will somehow make a man out of me. Besides, if I'm on the team, he gets to be assistant manager.

Mom has taught me to throw and catch and my real dad bought me a glove. Walt told me to swing the bat hard and level. Always, I have to keep my eye on the ball. Instead, always, I close my eyes when the ball comes speeding at me. Every pitch is aimed at my head.

My uniform itches something fierce. It's wool, just like real baseball players wear, and when you sweat from fear like I do, it prickles the skin on your arms and around your neck where your tee-shirt doesn't cover. My pants sag over my socks and I wear sneakers. One kid on the team, the coach's son and our star pitcher, has steel cleats. My shirt is the smallest size they make, but it's still too big for my thin body. The sleeves hang over my elbows.

Walt points at me and furrows his brow and I am unsure if he means to encourage me or to threaten me. I turn back to the pitcher. He winds up, fires the ball, and I flinch as the umpire calls a strike. I readjust my helmet and steal a glance at Walt. He's looking down at the ground shaking his head. I've never hit the ball during a game. I use the lightest bat in the team bag, but I just can't swing it fast enough to make contact with the moving ball because I know that ball is going to hit me and I have to be ready to duck. You can't duck and swing at the same time, Walt tells me this time and time again. Keep your eyes open and swing hard!

Walt raises his head and gives me a half-smile of indeterminate meaning. Maybe he's mocking me, I can't tell. He mimes a batter taking a stance and points to his feet. They are together, the left heel raised as if he's about to take a step. That's what he taught me and I've forgotten. When you stand that way, it's almost impossible to jump back from the ball. I nod and take that stance. The pitcher throws and I swing as hard as I can. No contact. Strike two. I missed by a mile. I don't know if the pitch was a ball or strike or even if the ball crossed the plate, much less how close my bat came to it. My eyes were closed.

I am not much good to the team. In the field, I seldom stop a grounder and never catch a fly and I can barely throw the ball all the way to first base from my position between second and third. The only reason I'm a starter at shortstop instead of a right-field sub is that Walt is the assistant manager.

Still, even though I have never actually hit the ball, I do get on base sometimes.

Walt calls time out and trots up to talk to me.

"You've got two strikes, David. Do you know what you are going to do on the next pitch?" I sigh. I nod. "Okay, for the team," he says. He pats me on the shoulder and hurries back to the coach's box. He didn't have to make such a big show of being the coach. I know what is expected of me. I have to get on base the only way I can. I don't want to, but there is no book I can lose myself in here, no place I can escape to on my bike, no way I can run outside the apartment to hide like I do at home when Mom begs him to get a job. In the batters' box, I have to face my fate.

I take my stance, bat raised, feet together just like I'm going to swing. I shuffle closer to the plate. Walt catches my eye and curls a finger as if beckoning me to him near first base. I inch still closer until my toes touch the white line of the batters' box. The blood rushes to my head and my knees quiver. As the pitcher winds up, I lean in over the plate. He throws and I close my eyes so I won't duck out of the way. I hope he doesn't hit me in the head. I twist into the ball's path and it hits me in the back of the arm in the fleshy part below the shoulder. It hurts, an explosive thump followed by a sharp ache. I cry and rub it as I walk to first base. I know I'm supposed to run, to shake it off, above all to not cry, but I have to. It hurts. It hit me in the same place I was hit yesterday.

~~§~~

I try not to coach Jeremy that way. He takes a pitch for a ball and I nod encouragement. It's the league championship game and we both really want to win since it is Jeremy's last season; mine, too. The batter ahead of him got to first with a sloppy single and represents the winning run. There is only one out and this is the bottom of the sixth inning, the last inning in the game, so we stand a good chance of winning. Double plays are very rare but passed balls are frequent, so as long as Jeremy can advance the runner, we can still win even if he makes a sacrificial out. It would be best if Jeremy can get on base, though, because the batter after him isn't very fast on the base path and Jeremy is. We have a play that requires heads-up base running, so we need Jeremy to reach first.

We've come a long way in the last seven years. When Jeremy turned six, Eileen insisted he sign up for Boy's Baseball, the organization that runs the game in the north end of New Rochelle where we live. Her brother and most of her cousins were fanatic softball players—even as adults—so it meant a lot to her. Given my experience with the game, I was ambivalent about it, but Jeremy wanted to play so I filled out the paperwork and sent it in.

We didn't hear anything and I more or less forgot about it until I spotted a headline in the *Standard Star*: "Boys' Baseball Parade to Start Season." What!? I called the guy who ran the league.

"I signed my son up two months ago but nothing happened. Is my boy on a team?" I demanded.

"If a coach didn't call you, no, he's not on a team," he said. "Sorry, but we don't have enough coaches. Your son's not the only one we can't accommodate." I didn't know how I was going to deliver that bad news to Jeremy or his mom. Then the guy added, "If you want to coach a team, your son can play." I couldn't tell if he was encouraging me or simply trying to brush me off. Without considering all the reasons why I couldn't or shouldn't do it, I said I would.

226

Jeremy and Eileen were excited. When the ramifications of what I had done soaked in, I wasn't so sure. I worked in Manhattan with a commute that took about an hour door to door. How was I going to get to a baseball field in New Rochelle before dark during the week? Speaking of fields, I didn't even know where they were located in town. My biggest worry, though, was how little I knew about the job I'd just taken on. I knew the rules of baseball (although the intricacies of the infield fly rule still escape me), but little more. My knowledge of the game's skills was rudimentary—I taught Jeremy to throw and catch and stop a grounder, but that was about it. How was I going to avoid making a fool of myself in front of a bunch of six- and seven-year-olds?

At the league president's house I picked up an equipment bag, a box of caps and shirts that said "Heaphy Cadillac" on them, and a couple of mimeographed pages that outlined the league rules. There weren't many. I also got a roster of players.

"Your first game is a week from Saturday," the president said. "You can use the field Tuesdays and Thursdays from five to seven for practice. Good luck."

Eileen helped call the parents on the roster to organize the first practice. I went to the library where I found a Little League coach's manual and a VHS videotape of baseball drills. Voila! I was a coach.

It was quite a team. Many of the kids were new to the game. They weren't exactly rejects, but they hadn't been put on a team to start with because, like Jeremy, the coaches didn't know them. We had the only girl in the league as well as her chubby little brother. They were born in India and had never seen, much less played, the game. The first time young Rakesh accidentally made contact between his bat and the ball, he ran from home to third base.

I made my share of rookie errors, too. I sent one of Jeremy's friends to play second base because he had a pretty good glove and could stop a grounder. I knew he was left-handed, but it didn't dawn on me it would slow down his throws to first base. I left him there anyway because Jeremy was playing first and I figured they would make it work because they played catch at home.

I also learned a few practical things they didn't put in the coach's manual. Right field, for example, is traditionally where you send your least adept fielder because it supposedly gets fewer hits. For seven-year-olds, though, it's just the opposite. Their swing speed isn't fast enough to get around on the ball and pull it into left like a major leaguer. They're more likely to slice the ball like a golfer with an open club face so the ball sails right. That's where your best fielder goes.

I also learned that every kid is afraid of the ball when they're batting, it's just that some hide their fear better than others.

Now, I watch as Jeremy swings and misses to even the count. It's okay, though, because his swing distracts the catcher, who lets the ball get past his legs and I send the runner to second base. If Jeremy gets on base, we'll have a chance to run the play.

"Eagle eye, Jeremy!" I call. "Make him pitch to you." Jeremy nods. He doesn't know about the play, but he knows what I mean.

Fred Massa is the manager and the play is his idea. Fred is a neighbor who has a daughter who is still too young to play ball. He loves the game, though, so he volunteers to coach the team. He does a good job of it, too, balancing the desire to win against the need to give the kids a positive sports experience. He's also a good buffer between Charlie and me. I don't know how I would have reacted if Charlie had taken over the manager's job. He lives with Eileen and the kids and is Fred's assistant coach. I'm just helping out at this game because we need a first base coach to run the play. Otherwise,

I'd be sitting in the stands watching Jeremy on the field like I have since Charlie moved in.

Jeremy watches the pitch go by high and outside just beyond the catcher's reach and the ball rolls to the backstop. Charlie is coaching third so he waves our runner to him.

At that moment, I didn't resent Charlie like I usually did. We're working as a team, he and I, and I am focused on the game. Actually, he's a good stepfather as far as I can tell. I think he gets along with Jeremy okay and he's uniquely suited to care for Leigh Anna. He has a sister with Down Syndrome and has aspirations of his own to become a special education teacher. What's not to like?

The next pitch is a strike and Jeremy swings. He knows if he gets a hit, our runner probably would score from third and the game would be over, but he fouls it off. I see the frustration in his eyes and sense a resolve to swing at the next pitch.

"Make 'em good," I yell. "Eagle eye!" He nods acknowledgement and digs his toe into the dirt. Jeremy is a good ball player. He knows his first job is to get on base. A hit would be sweet but a walk is safer. Jeremy knows.

He's played ball for seven years. I coached the first three as my marriage dissolved and the divorce wound down to its dreary end. Somewhere along the way, New Rochelle Boys Baseball fell apart, too, and Jeremy went to play on one of the Little League teams in the south end of town. They didn't need me. His Little League coach was a former high school star, maybe even a lower-rung minor leaguer at one time, who delighted in running up the score on the other team. The wins were nice and Jeremy got plenty of playing time, but it wasn't good to watch. I was happy when Boy's Baseball got organized again and Jeremy could play in a better environment. It stung when Eileen told me about it, though. Fred was going to coach and Charlie would be helping him. I was still in the stands.

Jeremy takes another ball and I give him a thumbs up. The count is full and the pitcher is tired. The catcher is, too, worn out by chasing wild pitches and his own passed balls. Jeremy isn't tired, though. He's pumped. I'm proud of him for keeping his emotions under control. He knows he could be a hero by getting a hit, but he's smart enough to know there's a chance of failure, too. Even a slim chance of disaster if he hits into a play that takes the runner out at home. A walk is a sure thing and he focuses on it. I don't tell him to protect the plate because he doesn't need the reminder.

I am very proud of Jeremy. Not as a baseball player, but as a person. He grows up to be a caring man, one who tends to a college roommate with a drinking problem and later tenderly nurses his mother on her death bed. He does the right thing when his first effort at self-employment fails; instead of declaring bankruptcy and walking away from his debts, he pays them off over time. He is patient and loving with his sister, which isn't always easy, and never shows a hint of jealousy at the extra attention she gets from us and others.

The next pitch is a ball in the dirt and Jeremy trots to first.

The play is on.

"Good job," I tell him. "Stick on the bag and don't go until I tell you, okay?" He nods. "Even if there's a wild pitch, don't run."

He looks at me quizzically, but says, "Okay, I got it."

We want the catcher to throw to second to try to get Jeremy out stealing. He won't do that if he has to chase the ball around the backstop. In this league, in order to give the defense a chance, runners can't take a lead off base until the pitch crosses the plate, so Jeremy stands on the bag while the pitcher winds up. He steps off with one foot as the pitcher throws, then fakes a run when the ball skids into the dirt under the catcher's glove. Jeremy comes back to first, disappointed that he couldn't steal second. I can't tell him why, though, because the first baseman is too close and will hear.

"That's the way," I say. "Wait for me."

I look across the diamond at Charlie. He's saying the same thing to his runner at third, I know. Charlie nods at me and we both look at Fred, who claps and shouts some fake encouragement to the batter. We don't want him to hit—a fly ball or a grounder to the pitcher could ruin the play and jeopardize the win.

The next pitch is perfect. The batter watches a strike, the ball pops safely into the catcher's mitt, and I tell Jeremy, "Go!"

He's surprised, but he streaks toward second. Both teams and the small crowd erupts. The catcher, surprised that a runner is actually trying to steal on him instead of just advancing safely on a passed ball, flips off his mask. He bobbles the ball a bit getting it out of his mitt, but fires the long throw to second.

As soon as the catcher rears back to throw, Charlie sends the runner from third. The play is a double steal. Timing is everything. It works perfectly. The throw to second goes to the wrong side of the bag and Jeremy slides in safe. The crowd noise rises as everyone realizes the runner from third is half way home. The throw from the startled second baseman doesn't get there in time and the runner scores. We win the championship.

The general celebratory confusion lasts several minutes and I get a chance to hug Jeremy as the melee settles down. I high five with Fred and Charlie. Everybody smiles broadly. Eileen and Leigh Anna join the small crowd of family members around the players as everyone drifts off toward the parking lot. My jubilation dies as they go. It's hard for me, but I have no choice but to watch my kids walk off with another man. The ball game is over.

1982

Afterword

Dreams are hard to remember. Even when you wake up the next morning intending to tell someone about them in all the dream's detail, you lose the vibrant realism as soon as you start talking about it. And the more bizarre those details are, the less sense the dream makes and the sooner you lose track of it. When I was twelve years old, I had a dream that stayed with me for the rest of my life because I never told anyone about it until now.

When it comes, I am sleeping by myself in my own room in the house on Jackson Street, the first house I have ever lived in. Lou didn't want Kenny sleeping in the same room with him and Mom and he was right—Ken was too big for that even though he was still in a crib. Mom moved him into the room Wayne and I shared, then moved her stuff out of her "sewing room" to make a bedroom for me. It's not only the first house I've ever lived in, it's the first room I've ever had to myself. My single bed even leaves room for a small desk where I can build model cars and do my homework.

This night I sleep well, soundly, tired from running outside all day, riding my bike, mowing the lawn, chasing around with the neighborhood kids until it's dark and the streetlights come on—and then a little longer until Lou whistles and I come in the house. I shower, I sleep.

In the deadest hour of the night, the time well past midnight after the moon has set but before the sky lightens with a hint of dawn, when the world is absolutely dark and still, I hear a footstep outside my room. I awaken, or at least I think I do.

I lie quiet, my head angled on my pillow so I can see out my bedroom door into the hall. I move not a hair though my heart races in my chest. I hear another soft step, slow, quiet, as if taken by a slippered foot. Silk slippers on a slim, elegant foot, I somehow know. Another step falls, barely audible on the carpeted floor. The hall gradually brightens. Someone is carrying a shaded candle to my room.

I dare not blink and I cannot move. My breath comes thankfully shallow, too quiet to draw notice. A hand carrying the candle moves past the door frame followed by a woman's gracious arm and then her erect figure draped in a diaphanous white gown that sweeps the floor. She turns to me, the toe of one silk slipper peeking beneath the hem of her gown. The candlelight shines in my eyes so I cannot see her face, but I know it is perfection. Her ethereal figure glows with a gentle light that comes not from the candle but from within. She does not speak, nor do I.

My head fills with a muffled regular ticking. Or maybe it is the slow, irrevocable drip, not from a leaking faucet, but from some ancient water clock. The sound tells me I have only so much time. This is death, I realize at that moment, and she will come for me. Not now, but sooner than I want. Now that I know how beautiful she is, I am not afraid.

I close my eyes. The light fades beyond my eyelids as her footfalls go past my room and down the hall. I go back to sleep, if indeed I have been awake, and remember this dream forever.

With Steve and Jeremy, 2017

Dave Donelson lives and writes in West Harrison, NY

Before he turned to freelance writing and photography, Dave Donelson enjoyed a career in broadcasting and other media that included positions as founder and/or president of four companies. He has also dedicated himself to public service in his community as president of the Westchester Library System, the Harrison Public Library and its foundation, and the Metropolitan Golf Writers Association.

Books by Dave Donelson

Non-fiction
Fathers: a Memoir
Creative Selling: Boost Your B2B Sales
The Dynamic Manager's Guide to Marketing & Advertising
The Dynamic Manager's Guide to Practical Management
The Dynamic Manager's Guide to Creative Selling
Slice-Free Golf by Brian Crowell (editor)

Fiction
Hunting Elf
Heart of Diamonds
Blind Curve
Weird Golf

Poetry/Photography
Manhattan Haiku

Made in the USA
Middletown, DE
26 August 2023

37356838R00146